For Alex, Annabelle and Giselle,

children of the Caribbean,

who may one day read it.

Acknowledgements

I am particularly grateful to James Ferguson for suggesting that I write this book, and to Jean McNeil and Liz Morrell at Latin America Bureau for seeing it through the press.

Faces of the Caribbean is based not only on conventional academic research, but also on many years of living and working in the Caribbean. A large part of it is the fruit of extensive travel in the region; much of this took place while I was working at *Caribbean Week*, and I am grateful to the publisher, Tim Forsythe, and to other colleagues at the paper for making this possible. Family and friends in Barbados, the many people I have met at different times in other parts of the region, and students and colleagues at the University of the West Indies and the University of Warwick have all contributed in various ways to shaping the ideas which inform these pages. A large part of whatever merits the book may possess is due to them — its faults are of course my own.

My wife Marita has given me constant encouragement and support over many years, and uncomplainingly endured my repeated absences. Our children have often wondered why their father was not around or was too busy to give them the attention he would have liked to have offered; this book is dedicated to them, in the hope that one day they may think at least some of it was worthwhile.

John Gilmore

Contents

The Caribbean

0   100   200   300   400   500 miles

0   100   200   300   400   500 kilometres

Atlantic Ocean

PUERTO RICO

San Juan

VIRGIN Is

ST CROIX

ANGUILLA

ST MARTIN/SINT MAARTEN

BARBUDA

ST KITTS

NEVIS

MONTSERRAT

ANTIGUA

GUADELOUPE

MARIE GALANTE

DOMINICA

MARTINIQUE

ST LUCIA

Bridgetown
BARBADOS

LEEWARD Is

WINDWARD Is

Lesser Antilles

ST VINCENT

GRENADA

BONAIRE

TOBAGO

Port of Spain
TRINIDAD

Caracas

Georgetown

Paramaribo

Cayenne

VENEZUELA

GUYANA

SURINAME

CAYENNE

BRAZIL

Introduction

Most people in North America and Europe think of the Caribbean not in terms of the sort of historical connection which their own countries have had with the region, but in terms of a handful of stereotypes and preconceived notions which are only slightly disturbed when some crisis like the Haitian boat people or Montserrat's volcano brings a part of the region to their television screens for a moment or two.

A long white beach fringed with palm trees ... Street festivals with colourful costumed bands and steel-pan music ... Triumphant fast-bowlers ... Dread-locked musicians ... For the British, the Caribbean tends to mean cricket, reggae music and package holidays; for Germans, the beach resorts of Puerto Plata on the north coast of the Dominican Republic; for the French, their own overseas departments of Martinique and Guadeloupe; for the Dutch, Curaçao or Aruba. For North Americans, a lot depends on where you live: if it's Miami, the Caribbean is Cuba, Fidel, and the community of Cuban-Americans centred around Calle Ocho; if it's New York City, you'll be more aware of Puerto Ricans and people from the Dominican Republic.

Of course there are Americans and Europeans who read the poetry of St. Lucia's Derek Walcott or Barbados' Kamau Brathwaite, or the novels of Trinidad's V. S. Naipaul or Martinique's Patrick Chamoiseau, who can tell the difference between reggae, zouk and kaiso music, and who can appreciate the merits of a fine old rum. But a lot of the time, for the rest of the world the Caribbean is a collection of rather small places a long way away, which are more or less interchangeable, as the post offices of Bermuda, the Bahamas and Barbados know to their cost. People in Dominica are accustomed to having their overseas mail missent to the Dominican Republic, and if you are writing to Guyana, it is a worthwhile precaution to put 'Guyana, South America' on the envelope, as otherwise your letter may end up in Ghana.

Yet the Caribbean is neither that small, or that far away. The islands lie around an arc which stretches for about 1,700 miles, or more than 2,700 kilometres, from Cabo de San Antonio at the western end of Cuba to Corozal Point on the north-western coast of Trinidad. If we take the common definition of the region as including all the islands from the Bahamas and Cuba in the north to Trinidad in the south, as well as those of Aruba, Bonaire and Curaçao to the north of Venezuela, together with the Guianas (Guyana, Suriname, French Guiana) and Belize, but excluding the other

1

mainland territories of South and Central America which have a coastline on the Caribbean Sea, we have a total population of between 37 and 38 million – or about a quarter as much again as the population of Canada (c. 30 million), or nearly four times that of Belgium (c. 10 million).

There are some millions of people of Caribbean origin and descent living outside of the Caribbean, in most of the major cities of North America and western Europe, as well as scattered in many less obvious places. Puerto Ricans in the United States, for example, may number as many as two million. For anyone living in London or Birmingham, Paris or Montreal or Toronto, Miami, New York or Boston, the Caribbean may well be in the next street. The Caribbean affects the music the citizens of 'metropolitan' areas listen to, the food they eat, the sports they play or watch, and where they take their holidays. Less attractive, but just as important, are the ways in which some of what happens in the Caribbean affects the supplies of the narcotics some of them consume, and the conduct of international financial services and other economic activities on which we all directly or indirectly depend.

From the 16th century to the early 20th century, European countries made money from slavery and indentured labour in the Caribbean; today the region is still a significant reservoir of cheap labour and cheap commodities for Europe and North America. As the USA discovered with successive groups of Cuban and Haitian immigrants, problems in the Caribbean today can easily become some bigger country's problem tomorrow. Yet people from the Caribbean living 'up North' are continually astounded by how little their neighbours know about them – many a Barbadian living in Britain or the United States has been put out by a doubtless well-intentioned inquiry as to which part of Jamaica he or she comes from. Millions of North Americans and Europeans visit the Caribbean as tourists every year, but a large proportion seldom venture beyond the beach, the poolside bar, and the areas devoted to duty-free shopping. At the same time, it has to be admitted that, while travel within the region has increased considerably within the last twenty-five or thirty years, there are still many people born, raised and living in the Caribbean who may have visited London and New York, or gone to Caracas for a shopping trip, but who have never been to another Caribbean island.

All over the world, the promotion of tourism tends to produce simplistic and misleading clichés. But some years ago, the Jamaica Tourist Board came up with a slogan that re-stated a fact which is too easily forgotten both by visitors to the region and by many of those in the Caribbean whose livelihood depends on the constant influx of outsiders – 'We're more than a beach, we're a country.'

This book is written in the belief that this is true of the Caribbean as a whole, and aims to give an overview of the region, and of the complex historical forces which have shaped the extraordinary diversity and creativity it possesses today. Not only is this diversity of interest in itself, but a better knowledge of the Caribbean has something to offer all of us, both Caribbean people and citizens of a larger world. Much of the story of the Caribbean is one of a shared legacy of endurance and triumph over hardship which has, in spite of all the divisive forces, in spite of all the hanging back of politicians reluctant to give up their status as big fish in small ponds, created what the Barbadian calypsonian Anthony 'Gabby' Carter describes as 'One People, One Nation.'

All you need to know?

Most of us have learnt to treat travel agents' brochures and similar promotional material with a certain amount of scepticism. But the industry keeps putting out this kind of stuff because it works – millions of us keep buying tickets to those exotic, faraway destinations because we're convinced this will give us a better time than saving our money and spending our holidays at home. And once we've done that, we have an investment in wanting to stay convinced. If you've been won over by the sort of copy to be found on one internet site aimed at potential tourists which refers to the Caribbean as 'hundreds of tropical isles some call paradise' and 'the No 1 playground for the Americas', you're not going to spend too much time on your holiday looking for anything which will spoil that image.

And it is a very powerful image, which turns up even in reference works which you might have thought were not out to sell you a vacation in paradise. The 1997 edition of *Compton's Interactive World Atlas*, a CD-ROM publication widely distributed in North America and Europe, includes a 30-second video captioned 'Caribbean and Central America: "One of the World's Most Popular Winter Resorts".' This begins with an aerial view of an island from the sea, with a few yachts visible in a picturesque bay of the sort the voice-over assures you is characteristic of the region. We are told that 'many islanders make their living by fishing', and we are shown fishing scenes: an old man with a cigarette and a broad-brimmed straw hat, people hauling nets in from the shore. The rest of the voice-over emphasises the importance of tourism, while we see brief shots of a street-vendor surrounded by children, and of school-children playing while wearing the school uniforms which Caribbean people all over the region take for granted, but which outsiders – particularly from North America – tend to think quaint.

The video ends as the voice-over gives way to steel-band music and we watch a steel-band playing on a beach.

None of this is actually untrue – you can see scenes like this in many parts of the Caribbean. But it is the only video about the region on the CD, and it does leave out a great deal. There is no mention of agriculture, manufacturing or of any service industries apart from tourism. There is not a glimpse of a modern building – not even a hotel. The still photographs in the same publication do little to redress the balance, showing a bias towards the more touristy destinations: Suriname and Guyana get one picture each, while there are more than twenty of the Bahamas, for example. Some of the pictures are miscaptioned: what is supposed to be 'Nassau Harbor' in the Bahamas is actually the Careenage in Bridgetown, Barbados; Antigua is supplied with a volcano and two architectural shots which may be somewhere in Latin America but are certainly not in that Caribbean island; and the caption of one of the pictures of the Dominican Republic refers to 'Ciudad Trujillo', which Santo Domingo has not been called since 1961.

A number of the text articles are of good quality, but several show inaccuracies or a failure to keep them up to date. It has not been true for several years that 'There is no television' in Guyana. The statement that 'a French patois is also widely spoken' in St. Vincent suggests that somebody has confused that island with St. Lucia. Similar inaccuracies are to be found in other current guide-books or works of reference and demonstrate that all too often where tourism is concerned, creating a favourable impression takes precedence over the facts.

4

1. Imperial legacies

Open the map. More islands there, man,
Than peas on a tin plate, all different size...

As many islands as the stars at night...

Derek Walcott, 'The Schooner *Flight* – 11: After the Storm',
from *The Star-Apple Kingdom* (1979)

'An emporium for all the world'

If you get up at dawn on a fine day in Oranjestad, the capital of St. Eustatius in the Netherlands Antilles, and walk the road which runs along Gallows Bay, the sea – only a few yards away – has that pale, almost turquoise blue familiar from a thousand picture-postcards and tourist brochures of destinations all over the Caribbean. Although there is a beach of the same picture-postcard splendour a little further on, there is no beach right here: the sea washes onto rocks whose presence here is not natural, for every so often a low, broken wall protrudes from them.

The rocks come from the ruins of the stone- and brick-built warehouses which lined the bay two hundred years ago when St. Eustatius (or Statia, as even then it was more popularly known) was one of the busiest ports in the Americas, 'a place of vast traffick from every quarter of the globe,' and the island's population of over eight thousand was more than four times what it is today.

There are few complete buildings here in Oranjestad's Lower Town today, but the warehouses once stretched for a mile and a half along the bay, filled with 'rich embroideries, painted silks, flowered Muslins, with all the Manufactures of the Indies ... exquisite silver plate ... iron pots, kettles and shovels ... excellent French gloves for fourteen pence a pair, also English thread-stockings cheaper than I could buy them at home,' as a Scottish 'lady of quality' called Janet Schaw noted in 1775, although she did not mention the 'slave house' which had been built in the early 18th century, large enough to secure 450 slaves brought from Africa while they awaited resale and transport to other Caribbean islands or even to North America. Trade brought so much prosperity to Statia that its eight square miles became

Gallows Bay, St. Eustatius, a busy port in the 18th century   *John Gilmore*

known as the 'Golden Rock' and something to be fought over by the European colonisers of the Caribbean; the island changed hands 22 times between the French, the Dutch and the British before it became Dutch for good in 1816.

Turning off the road, a broad steep footpath known as the Bay Road or, less prosaically, as the Slave Walk in tribute to those who built it in 1803, leads to the Upper Town.   Here you can find a mixture of modern and older buildings including Fort Oranje, which dates back to the 17th century. Its bastions stand on the edge of the cliff, overlooking the Lower Town and the sea. It was here, on 16 November 1776, the island's Dutch commander, Johannes de Graaff, ordered the fort's cannon to fire a salute in return of one from the brig *Andrew Doria* of the navy of the Continental Congress. The *Andrew Doria* was flying the Grand Union Flag (not the Stars and Stripes, which did not come into use until nearly seven months later) and the salute ordered by de Graaff is generally recognised as the first ever given by an official of a foreign power to a flag of what later became the United States of America.

The salute led to a formal diplomatic protest from Britain to the Netherlands.   More important was the fact that Statia was the source of a large proportion of the munitions and ordinary supplies reaching the North American rebels, and a British fleet under Admiral Rodney occupied and plundered the island in February 1781.   Statia recovered, but the end of the slave trade and the decline of the island's importance as an entrepôt

6

(trans-shipment port) as a result of the independence of the United States and the French Revolutionary and Napoleonic wars had destroyed its prosperity by the beginning of the 19th century. The warehouses in the Lower Town were allowed to decay, and many buildings were demolished for the sake of the thin red and yellow bricks which had originally been imported from Holland as ballast, and which were now re-exported to provide a little income for Statia's much diminished population. The cannon which had fired the 'First Salute' also vanished, perhaps sold as scrap to some visiting entrepreneur.

Wandering out through the Upper Town – perhaps passing the yellow brick ruins of Honen Dalim ('He who is merciful to the poor'), built in 1739, the second oldest synagogue in the Americas, or the stone walls of the Dutch Reformed Church, roofless since 1792 – you come into countryside so dry you realise why many of the houses in the town stand beside huge old cisterns built to store whatever rain can be collected. A little later, you can be climbing the slopes of the Quill, as the extinct volcano which dominates the island's landscape is known, apparently from the Dutch *de Kuil*, 'the pit'. About half-way up, there is a magnificent view of most of the island, including Oranjestad and the modern village of Golden Rock, founded in 1974 near both the airport and a pre-Columbian Amerindian site. You are now climbing a steep path through thick trees and vegetation, meeting butterflies, hermit crabs and, if you are lucky, one of the beautiful and harmless brown and gold snakes which make their home among the dead leaves which cover the soil. At the rim of the volcano, you can climb down into the thickly-forested crater or carry on round and up until you reach the highest point, Mazinga, after a strenuous walk which has taken you the best part of five hours from the sea-shore. You may be rewarded by a view of the neighbouring island of St. Kitts to the south-east, or, since Mazinga is nearly 2,000 feet (600 metres) above sea-level, you may be able to see nothing but cloud.

The historical legacy is perhaps more obvious there than in some other places, but St. Eustatius is in many ways a miniature of the Caribbean: the natural beauty and the attractions of historic buildings go with a grim past. The island has had to depend in one way or another on the outside world for nearly 400 years. In the 18th century it made itself into 'an emporium for all the world; a mart, a magazine for the nations of the earth,' in the words of the Irish philosopher and politician Edmund Burke. In more modern times it has become a tourist destination, wooing visitors from North America to the Franklin Delano Roosevelt Airport, named for a president who in 1939 got no nearer to the island than the deck of a passing US naval vessel.

The 'First Salute' has become an important resource, and it makes a good story, suggesting how 'America's Childhood Friend' (as the tourist literature sometimes refers to Statia) helped in the birth of democracy and New World freedom from Old World tyranny. At the same time, one of Statia's main selling points is scuba diving, and divers and beachcombers alike are encouraged to search for the five-sided blue glass beads which are still occasionally to be found washed up by the Lower Town or under water just offshore after heavy seas. Once common here, and seldom, if ever, found anywhere else, they have become something of a Statian icon; visitors are told that they used to be used in the slave trade.

The Netherlands was never a major colonial power in the region, but the Dutch flag still flies over six islands in the Caribbean, and if you chose any six islands at random, it would be hard to find more variety. Just north of Statia, and within sight of it, is Saba, whose five square miles consist almost entirely of a single volcanic cone rising so steeply from the sea that there is scarcely anything resembling a beach to be found. Landing at Fort Bay in the days of sea travel used almost always to involve a soaking, though there are now better harbour facilities, and the island has an airport, opened in 1963, with what is claimed to be the shortest runway in regular commercial use in the world. Landing there is an experience, as the airport takes up virtually all the flat land in the island, and there are cliffs on three sides.

In spite of this, and the lack of beaches, Saba attracts considerable numbers of tourists, drawn mainly by the excellent diving and the variety of underwater life which results from the fact that the island's coastal waters have been a protected marine park for many years. From the village of Windwardside you can walk to the top of the aptly named Mount Scenery; at nearly 3,000 feet above sea-level, it is a lot higher than Mazinga, but a well-made path with a thousand or so steps makes it an easier ascent – Queen Beatrix of the Netherlands is said to have done it in high heels. The path leads through cloudforest which is home to some species found nowhere else, such as the Saba lizard, which has chocolate-coloured spots on an orange skin.

Unlike Statia, which once had more than seventy plantations, Saba was never a sugar island. Before the advent of tourism, Sabans made their living from subsistence agriculture, from fishing and boat-building, and from service in the navies of the world. Even here, however, slavery has left its mark. While the population of Statia is almost entirely black, that of Saba is almost equally divided between black and white. It is a strange experience for a visitor from somewhere like Barbados to get up on a Sunday morning in Windwardside and realise that he is in a village in the Caribbean

8

Cloudforest in Saba,
Netherlands Antilles

John Gilmore

and that every one of the people he sees going to church is white. Visitors are assured that racial divisions in Saba are not what they once were, but it is still the case that the island's population (about 1100) is divided between two predominantly white villages and two predominantly black ones.

The cultural mosaic

Fifteen minutes by a small plane from both Statia and Saba is Sint Maarten, the third of the territories in what are called the Dutch Windward Islands, although they are the north-eastern Caribbean, in the middle of what most English-speaking people in the Caribbean call the Leeward Islands. The Dutch Leeward Islands, on the other hand, are a little over five hundred miles away to the south-west, within sight of the coast of Venezuela. They are sometimes called the ABC islands, though from west to east Aruba, Curaçao and Bonaire lie in that order. Here there is no cloudforest: the highest point, the Christoffelberg in Curaçao, is only 375 metres (1230 feet), and most of the landscape of the three islands is low-lying, arid, and characterised by an abundance of cactus and the divi-divi trees whose tops are bent over almost at right-angles by the prevailing winds.

They may share the Dutch flag and a – quite recent – dependence on tourism, but the six islands of the Dutch Caribbean differ in more than location and climate. They are no longer a political unit. After many years of complaining of what it saw as the unfair dominance of Curaçao (the largest and most populous of the islands), in 1986 Aruba broke away from the Netherlands Antilles, an internally self-governing federation established in 1954 to replace the islands' former colonial status. In a 1993 referendum, the remaining five islands voted to keep together, but the smaller ones continue to feel that the federation is dominated by Curaçao and, to a lesser extent, by Sint Maarten. Dutch continues to be taught in the islands' schools, because for most Arubans and Antilleans higher education still means study in the Netherlands, but natives of the Dutch Windward Islands have English as their mother tongue, while the vernacular of the ABC islands is Papiamentu, a creole language which is to a large extent based on Spanish. Even here there are divisions, for in Aruba the language is somewhat closer to Spanish, while there is more of a Dutch influence in Curaçao; Arubans refuse to use the standardised orthography developed in Curaçao, and the two territories cannot even agree on how to spell the name of the language they share – it is Papiamento in Aruba and Papiamentu in Curaçao and Bonaire. The people of Curaçao and Bonaire are predominantly black, while most Arubans are of mixed Amerindian and European ancestry, although Aruba does have a significant black community mostly immigrants from the Eastern Caribbean and their descendants who still live mainly in the town of San Nicolas near the oil refinery whose demand for labour brought them there.

Other attractions, particularly the tourism and offshore industries, have brought representatives of dozens of different nationalities to live in Curaçao and Aruba, and many of the inhabitants are fluent in Dutch, Spanish and English as well as Papiamentu. But the most obviously cosmopolitan of the Dutch Caribbean territories is Sint Maarten. Almost every visitor to the island hears some version of the legend of how Saint Martin/Sint Maarten was divided between the Dutch and the French in 1648: a Dutchman and a Frenchman walked round the island in opposite directions, with the frontier to be fixed where they met. The Dutchman fortified himself for the task with gin, while the Frenchman drank nothing stronger than wine, with the result that the Frenchman walked further and the French got the larger, northern section of the island. Ever since, one is usually told, the two nations have lived in amity, which is not quite accurate.

10

Table 1: Population by country (1999 estimate)

Country	Population (1999)	Country	Population (1999)
Anguilla	11,510	Guyana	705,156
Antigua & Barbuda	64,246	Haiti	6,884,264
Aruba	68,675	Jamaica	2,652,443
Bahamas	283,759	Martinique	411,539
Barbados	259,751	Netherlands Antilles*	207,827
Belize	235,789	Puerto Rico	3,887,652
British Virgin Islands	19,156	St. Kitts & Nevis	42,838
Cayman Islands	39,335	St. Lucia	154,020
Cuba	11,096,395	St. Vincent and the Grenadines	120,519
Dominica	64,881	Suriname	431,156
Dominican Republic	8,129,734	Trinidad & Tobago	1,102,096
French Guiana	167,982	Turks & Caicos Islands	16,863
Grenada	97,008	US Virgin Islands	119,827
Guadeloupe	420,943	(*Curaçao, Bonaire, Sint Maarten, Saba, Sint Eustatius)	

Source: CIA World Factbook

Nevertheless, the fact that the island was small and devoid of natural resources (except for the salt pond in the Dutch section) ensured that for much of its history the island was a sleepy backwater. Tobacco, sugar and cotton were grown at different periods, but the island was never of any significance as an exporter of agricultural produce. Statia, not Sint Maarten, enjoyed its period of prosperity as the region's great entrepôt, because the skippers of merchant vessels preferred the open roadstead of Statia to the bays of Sint Maarten, which were obstructed by shallows. Even in 1960, there were less than 5,000 people in the French and Dutch parts together, and it was not long since a shareholder of the power company in Philipsburg, the capital of the Dutch part, had questioned the suggestion that current should be supplied up to 11 o'clock at night, asking 'What self-respecting person would want an electric bulb shining in his home after 10 p.m.!'

Change came after the 1959 revolution in Cuba left large numbers of American tourists looking for alternative destinations in the Caribbean.

Several entrepreneurs saw opportunities in Sint Maarten and the number of hotel rooms in the Dutch part went from 60 in 1960 to over 700 in 1970 and over 2000 by 1982. Where Dutch Sint Maarten had taken the initiative, French St. Martin followed, and both sections have long been equally keen on drawing visitors. The usual attractions of a Caribbean holiday were supplemented by Philipsburg's status as a free port, which brought shoppers from many other Caribbean territories, as well as North American tourists. The availability of casino gambling on the Dutch side later became another attraction for many visitors.

The tourist boom led to large-scale development, often with little attention to planning or environmental concerns, and to a demand for workers which was filled by substantial immigration, in some cases that of returning locals who had emigrated to Curaçao, Aruba, or elsewhere in search of work in previous decades. Even so, a large proportion of jobs in the expanding economy, at all levels from manual workers to owners of businesses, was taken by complete newcomers to the island. Significant illegal immigration made nonsense of official statistics, but some estimates put the island's population as high as sixty or even eighty thousand by the early 1990s, with perhaps as little as 20% being native St.-Martiners.

Visitors who ventured beyond their hotel beach or the duty-free shops on Philipsburg's Front Street could find an island with two governments, two different electricity and telephone systems, two official currencies trying to maintain a presence in competition with the ubiquitous circulation of the US dollar, a choice of several flags (the French and Dutch tricolors, the flag of the Department of Guadeloupe to which the French side belongs, the flags of the Netherlands Antilles and the Island Territory of Sint Maarten, plus a number of unofficial flags proposed by various groups including advocates of a united and independent St. Martin). There are at least seven languages in common use – the official French and Dutch, the English which has been the language of the native St.-Martiners at least since the end of the 18th century, the French Creole of immigrants from Guadeloupe and Martinique, the rather different Creole spoken by immigrants from Haiti, the Papiamento spoken by officials sent by the federal government of the Netherlands Antilles in Curaçao and by other permanent or temporary immigrants from the ABC islands, and the Spanish of immigrants from the Dominican Republic – all of this in an island of only 37 square miles. The destruction caused by Hurricane Luis in 1995 was used as an excuse by authorities on both the French and Dutch sides to round up and deport large numbers of illegal immigrants for whom, it was said, they were unable to provide, but the infrastructure of the tourist industry was rapidly rebuilt, and it was soon business as usual on the island.

12

Guyanese Amerindians
as pictured in a locally-
produced postcard,
c1900

Courtesy of John Gilmore

A vanished people

Saint Martin/Sint Maarten may be an extreme example, but the legacies of the past have turned the entire Caribbean into a racial and cultural mosaic. Once the region was occupied by indigenous Amerindian peoples who differed among themselves in language and to some extent in customs, but who shared a broad cultural similarity perhaps best symbolised by the divine origin they attributed to the cassava plant (*Manihot esculenta*) – the great staple of Amerindian culture from Cuba to the Amazon.

The arrival of Columbus was disastrous for the Amerindians in 1492. Some Spanish engaged in deliberate massacre of the Amerindian population, but more destructive was the collapse of indigenous methods of agriculture brought about by Spanish demands for forced labour, and the introduction of European diseases to which the Amerindians had no resistance. Historians continue to argue about the causes and the numbers involved, but there is no disputing the fact that within no more than 50 years of the establishment of European settlement in the Caribbean the indigenous population of the Greater Antilles had been almost entirely wiped out. The smaller islands of the Eastern Caribbean provided a refuge for a little

13

longer, but Spanish slave raids in the 16th century and the later encroachments of other European powers took their toll and by the end of the 18th century the survivors of the 'first peoples' had been reduced to a small group in one corner of Dominica and a tiny remnant in Trinidad.

Descendants of these two groups survive to the present day and continue the struggle to preserve their cultural heritage. In St. Vincent, the Amerindians are represented by descendants of the Black Caribs, a group of mixed Amerindian and African heritage which became famous for its resistance to British encroachment on their lands, but many of the Black Caribs were deported from St. Vincent by the British at the end of the 18th century. The descendants of the deportees became the Garifuna people, now found in Belize, Honduras and Nicaragua, a group which seems predominantly or exclusively of African descent in appearance, but who have preserved much of the linguistic and cultural heritage of their Amerindian ancestors. In the southern Caribbean, the entire Amerindian population of Aruba, Curaçao and Bonaire was deported to Hispaniola by the Spaniards in 1515. A few later returned to Aruba, where they were reinforced by later Amerindian immigrants from the Venezuelan mainland, but although many of today's Arubans are of partly Amerindian descent, the last pure-blooded Amerindian in the island is said to have died in 1862. In Guyana, mid-19th-century observers believed the Amerindians to be on the verge of extinction, but they have managed to survive and even increase in numbers, so that Amerindian peoples from nine separate groups form perhaps 5% of the country's total population. But even in Guyana the Amerindians are socially and economically marginalised, and some Amerindian groups, such as the Pianoghottos, who were still to be found in the middle of the 19th century, no longer exist in the country.

War and colonisation

Throughout the 16th century the monopoly which the Spanish had established in the Caribbean was effective, but not unchallenged. The much-quoted remark of François Ier, King of France, that he would like to see the clause in Adam's will which excluded him from a share in the world, was followed up by frequent raids by French corsairs on Spanish territories in the Caribbean and attacks on Spanish shipping returning from the New World. Later John Hawkins pioneered not only English incursions into the Caribbean, but also English involvement in the slave trade from Africa to the New World. Hawkins traded with the Spanish colonists – contrary to the regulations of their own government – whenever he could, and attacked them when he couldn't. His successes brought him many rewards, including the grant of a coat of arms with, as its crest, the figure of 'a

Negro, manacled.' Like Hawkins, Francis Drake saw expeditions to the Caribbean as both a source of wealth from trading and raiding, and a means of furthering his country's cause in the conflicts between England and Spain in Europe. Similarly, when the Dutch began to wage a war of independence against their Spanish masters, they found it both profitable and strategically valuable to extend the struggle into Caribbean waters.

From the early 17th century, other European powers succeeded in establishing settlements in parts of the Caribbean where neither the Spanish nor the surviving indigenous inhabitants were capable of keeping them out. A few minor players were involved, generally only for brief periods – the Knights of Malta, the Brandenburgers, and the Dukes of Courland from what is now Latvia, who sent several groups of settlers to Tobago over a period of some fifty years, and who maintained a nominal claim to the island into the 18th century. The Danes established themselves in the Virgin Islands towards the end of the 17th century, and as late as 1784 the Swedes acquired a Caribbean colony in the form of the small island of St. Bartholomew, which was ceded to them by the French (to whom they sold it again in 1877).

But by the time of the Treaty of Ryswick in 1697, when Spain formally ceded the western portion of the island of Hispaniola to France, a pattern had been established with consequences which have proved to be long-lasting. The Spanish kept Cuba, Puerto Rico, the eastern portion of Hispaniola, and a sleepy outpost in Trinidad, which they finally lost to the British in 1797. The British retained Jamaica, which they had captured from the Spanish in 1655. Most of the Eastern Caribbean fell to the French and the British, while the Dutch made up for the smallness of their island territories by the importance of Curaçao and Statia as trading centres and by their mainland plantation colonies in the Guianas.

The Caribbean was an important theatre of war in successive European conflicts, and some islands changed hands several times before the end of the Napoleonic Wars in 1815 saw a final redistribution of the region's territories between the British, the French and the Dutch. A long and fiercely-fought revolution had achieved the independence of Haiti in 1804, and with it Spain's loss of control over eastern Hispaniola – a loss which, with one brief interval, proved to be permanent.

The United States of America had had important trading interests in the Caribbean since long before their own war of independence, but did not formally acquire any territorial interests in the region until their victory in the Spanish-American War of 1898 gave them Puerto Rico and de facto control of a nominally independent Cuba. They followed this up with the acquisition of the Panama Canal Zone in 1904 and, in 1917, by the purchase

15

of the Danish West Indies, which became the United States Virgin Islands. It was not until after the Second World War that important changes came about in the constitutional relations between France and the Netherlands and their respective Caribbean territories, and not until the period following the 1960s that most of the British colonies in the region moved to independence.

The influence of the Spanish, the British, the French, and the Dutch in the Caribbean has been long-lasting and profound, not least in the imposition of the linguistic divisions which have, on the one hand, contributed to the fascinating cultural variety of the region and, on the other, been a major factor in its continuing fragmentation and disunity in the face of external pressures. But of course the Caribbean is not, and never has been, a simple extension of Europe. The Amerindians may have declined all too rapidly into virtual extinction, but not before they had time to make some impact on the culture of their destroyers, an impact which still lingers, albeit a little stronger in some places than in others. And all except the smallest European colonies were never for more than brief periods colonies of settlement, in the sense of being places inhabited solely or almost entirely by groups of people from Europe. It was only ten years after the first voyage of Columbus that the first enslaved Africans were brought to Hispaniola, and from then on all the colonising powers enforced, encouraged, or merely permitted the migration into the Caribbean of groups of peoples from practically every corner of the globe.

For centuries the descendants of Africans have been found throughout the region, and they have long been numerically predominant in much of it, although the descendants of a later migration of indentured labourers from India are now the largest ethnic group in Guyana and Trinidad, as well as being found in several other territories, such as Jamaica, Guadeloupe and Suriname. There are significant Chinese communities in Cuba, Jamaica, Trinidad and Suriname; you can find Javanese in Suriname and Hmongs from Cambodia in French Guiana, and more than one Caribbean country has had a head of state or head of government of Lebanese descent.

The fate of the Amerindians, the long periods of armed conflict between different colonial powers, the voluntary and involuntary movements of peoples into the region, all had a common cause. Ever since the fateful day of 12 October 1492 the Caribbean has been seen as a source of wealth, not, for the most part, for the benefit of people living in the region, but for the enrichment of outsiders.

2. The riches of the earth

I watched carefully to discover whether they had gold and saw that some of them carried a small piece hanging from a hole pierced in the nose. I was able to understand from their signs that to the south, either inland or along the coast, there was a king who had large vessels made of it and possessed a great deal. [...] So I resolved to go south-west to seek the gold and precious stones.

From Columbus' account of his first encounters with the Amerindians of the Bahamas, 13 October 1492 (translated by J. M. Cohen).

This *Martynes* was he that christened the citie of *Manoa*, by the name of *El Dorado* [...] Those *Guianians* and also the borderers, and all others in that tract which I have seen are maruelons great drunkardes, in which vice I think no nation can compare with them and at the times of their solemne feasts when the Emperor carowseth with his Captayns, tributories, & governours, the manner is thus. All those that pledge him are first stripped naked, & their bodies annoynted al ouer with a kinde of white *Balsamum*: by them called *Curcai*) of which there is great plenty and yet very deare amongst them, and it is of all other the most pretious, whereof we have had good experience; when they are annointed all ouer, certaine seruants of the Emperor hauing prepared gold made into fine powder blow it thorow hollow canes vpo[n] their naked bodies, vntill they be al shining from the foote to the head, & and in this sort they sit drinking by twenties and hundreds & continue in drunkennes sometimes sixe or seuen daies togither [...] Vpon this sight, and for the abundance of gold which he saw in the citie, the Images of gold in their Temples, the plates armors, and shields of gold which they vse in the wars, he called it *El Dorado*.

Sir Walter Raleigh, *The Discoverie of the Large, Rich, and Bewtiful Empyre of Gviana, With a relation of the great and Golden Citie of Manoa (which the Spanyards call El Dorado)* ... (London, 1596)

Colonel *James Drax*, whose beginning upon that Iland, was founded upon a stock not exceeding 300 l. sterling, has raised his fortune to such a height, as I have heard him say, that he would not look towards England, with a purpose to remain there, the rest of his life, till he were able to purchase an estate of ten thousand pound land yearly; which he hop'd in few years to accomplish, with what he was then owner of; and all by this plant of Sugar. Colonel *Thomas Modiford*, has often told me, that he had taken a Resolution to himself, not to set his face for England, til he had made his voyage, and imployment there, worth him an hundred thousand pounds sterling; and all by this Sugar plant. And these, were men of as percing sights, and profound judgments, as any I have known in that way of management. Now if such Estates as these, may be raised, by the well ordering this plant, by Industrious and painful men, why may not such estates, by careful keeping, and orderly and moderate expending, be preserv'd, in their posterities, to the tenth Generation, and by all the sweet Negotiation of Sugar?

Richard Ligon, *A True & Exact History of the Island of Barbadoes* (2nd ed., London, 1673)

Profit for plunder

Towards the end of his life Columbus became something of a mystic, and appears to have believed that in some way his discoveries would lead to Christendom's recovery of the Holy Places of Palestine from the Turks. He also made much of the idea that his voyages would bring about the saving of souls, as a result of the conversion of the pagans they encountered. Nevertheless, it is clear that his main selling proposition, the one which convinced his royal patrons, King Ferdinand of Aragon and his wife Queen Isabella of Castile to give him the backing in ships and men which he needed, was the very practical one that exploration could be profitable.

Earlier Portuguese voyages along the coast of Africa had already shown this to be the case, and, out in the Atlantic, the Azores, Madeira, the Canary and Cape Verde Islands, had all been claimed and to some extent settled by the Portuguese and the Spanish, with commercially successful results. We can forget the old yarn about how Columbus was long denied an opportunity by obscurantists who thought the earth was flat. All educated people were well aware of the spherical nature of the earth, and their objections to Columbus' scheme for opening up a new way to the riches of Far Eastern trade were based on a correct opinion that the globe was considerably larger than he claimed it was – if the 'New World' had not proved to be in the

Columbus and the first encounter   *Engraving by Theodor de Bry, 1590*

way, given the ships available to him, Columbus and his men would have
starved to death long before they got to China or Japan.

In 1492 Ferdinand and Isabella had taken Granada and completed the
recapture of Spain from the Muslims who had occupied much of the Iberian
peninsula for seven centuries. Columbus got what he wanted because he
was persistent – he had been trying his luck in Spain for about ten years –
and because he was in effect offering Ferdinand and Isabella something for
nothing. As the modern historian Felipe Fernández-Armesto has pointed
out, licences to explore the Atlantic were easy to come by (eight survive in
the Portuguese archives for the period 1462 to 1487), and the Crown did
not put up any ready money at all: it did supply about half the total cost of
the voyage, but even this was supplied by two officials 'against expectations
from the sale of indulgences and, in fact, it was all recovered in due course
from the proceeds of sales in a poor diocese of Extremadura.' Queen Isabella's
pawning her jewels is another traditional story we can forget.

From the first day Columbus arrived in the New World, setting foot on
the island in the Bahamas he called San Salvador on 12 October 1492, his
account of his discoveries makes clear the importance of commercial
considerations. The Amerindians seemed to him 'a people short of
everything', but they 'should be good servants' and he took some of them
back to Spain with him 'so that they can learn to speak' – an ominous
foreshadowing of the ruthless exploitation of Amerindian labour. He spoke

19

Panning for gold, Suriname, early 20th century   *Courtesy of John Gilmore*

of the beauty of the islands, of how the climate was like April in Andalusia, and of the marvellous variety of trees and fruits, about which wishful thinking made him declare: 'I am certain they are all valuable.' Above all, the natives possessed gold. It was no more than a few ornaments, but Columbus persuaded himself that he understood the natives to confirm that more gold was to be had in the region, always somewhere not very far away.

It was enough to ensure that there would be more voyages. Whatever the strength of the claims put forward on behalf of mediaeval Irish monks, or Viking explorers, or expeditions sent out by West African kings or Bristol merchants, however willing we are to admit the fallacies and ethnocentrism inherent in traditional references to 'the Discovery of the New World,' in the end it was that first transatlantic crossing by Columbus which mattered. Columbus not only went from Europe to the Americas; he made the return voyage and inaugurated regular and continuous contact between the two. As the modern Trinidadian Calypso singer Shadow put it, 'Columbus lie', and he lied very effectively, probably deceiving even himself, in presenting a seductive picture of the territories with which he had made contact as lands of opportunity, where vast wealth was to be had more or less for the asking, and where every Spanish adventurer could become a gentleman. The vision held just long enough for the Caribbean islands to serve as stepping-stones to the discovery and conquest of the less illusory riches of the mainland Americas.

As it turned out, there was indeed gold to be panned from the rivers or dug from the soil of Hispaniola and Cuba, and the native populations were soon being compelled to produce it, parcelled out among the settlers under the so-called *repartimiento* ('distribution') system, which differed from slavery in little more than name. The gold which was accessible to 16th-century technologies was exhausted within a few decades. By this time the Amerindians of the Greater Antilles had vanished into the pages of history, and the capture of Mexico by Cortez (1519-21), and of Peru by Pizarro (1530-1533) had given the Spanish far greater and seemingly inexhaustible sources of precious metals. The magnificent harbours of Havana and Santo Domingo gave them a continuing importance as ports of call – in 1574, Havana was visited by 101 ships from Spain and 115 from the colonies, and the coat of arms granted to the city in the 17th century bore three castles of silver and a golden key in recognition of its strategic value. Still, the Caribbean islands long remained economic backwaters in comparison with the prosperity of the mainland colonies.

The search for gold or silver or precious stones went on but, for the most part, with little result. The island of Margarita, off the coast of Venezuela, owed its name to a pearl-fishery which was soon exhausted. Deluded by a second-hand traveller's tale, Sir Walter Raleigh led two expeditions up the rivers of the Guianas in 1595 and 1617-8 in search of the imaginary golden city of El Dorado. He failed to find any significant quantities of gold and the annoyance he caused the Spanish ultimately cost him his head. In 1720 a group of speculators in England obtained a patent from King George I establishing themselves as the Gold and Silver Mines Co. of Jamaica, and succeeded in selling shares to the general public. It appears that a few miners were in fact sent to Jamaica to prospect for such mines, but the scheme collapsed in a succession of law-suits after one of the patentees invested the money which had been paid for shares in that much greater speculation of the time, the South Sea Bubble, just before it burst. Not surprisingly, disgruntled shareholders complained that the 'Project was a mere Imposture, there having been no Attempt to discover, or at the least Probability of discovering any Gold or Silver in Jamaica.'

The gold fever continued, and repeated efforts to locate mineral resources, combined with improvements in technology, eventually produced some successes. In 1824 gold was discovered in Aruba, and was exploited by commercial companies from 1854 to 1916, though over the entire period only a little under 3,000 pounds weight of gold was exported from the island. Discoveries in the 1840s revealed that Raleigh was right after all, and that there were significant quantities of gold in the Guianas - although no El Dorado. The discovery of diamonds followed later. The exploitation of gold mines continues to be important in both Guyana and Suriname, though there are serious ecological costs (see Chapter 5 below). There is also a modern gold mine in the Dominican Republic.

All that glitters

Less glittering mineral prizes have achieved prominence in national economies.

Jamaica, Guyana and Suriname are significant producers of bauxite, the ore from which both aluminium and alumina (aluminium oxide), which is used as a catalyst in petrochemical processes and for other industrial purposes, are produced. While other bauxite producers (such as Brazil, Australia and India) are highly competitive, the Caribbean industries remain important to the world market. In 1952 Reynolds Jamaica Mines Limited (a subsidiary of the Reynolds Metals Company of the USA) started to export kiln-dried ore. Alumina Jamaica Limited (a subsidiary of the Aluminium Company of Canada) began exporting alumina in 1953. By 1972 Jamaica had a total of five alumina plants and two bauxite drying plants with a combined annual capacity of 15 million tonnes of bauxite. There has been some decline since then, but in the late 1990s Jamaica still had one bauxite and three alumina plants which together produced an annual average of some 11 million tonnes which accounted for just over 50% of the country's total exports.

Cuba is an important source of nickel. Trinidad is home to one of the world's older petroleum industries, with oil deposits being commercially exploited from before the First World War. The sharp rise in international prices in the 1970s gave the country a temporary oil boom and paid for the development of a number of related industries. The availability of salt-pans was one of the factors which brought the Dutch to the Caribbean from the late 16th century: the Great Salt Pond in Sint Maarten is now largely filled in and built over, but in Bonaire the salt industry was revived in the 1960s and that island now exports several hundred thousand metric tons of salt a year. From 1865 until 1914, the small island of Redonda in the Leewards (now uninhabited, and part of the territory of Antigua and Barbuda) was successfully mined for phosphates. During the same period phosphates were also mined in Aruba. In Barbados, a type of coal locally referred to as manjak was intermittently exploited from the 17th century until the 1920s, and one of the island's minor exports was a petroleum derivative known as 'Barbadoes tar' which was to be found in European pharmacopoeias into the 19th century on account of its alleged medicinal properties.

Oil platform, Trinidad   *Philip Wolmuth/Panos Pictures*

Fuelling growth: oil in Trinidad and Tobago

Although oil was first discovered in Trinidad in 1866, commercial development did not begin until 1908, with exports of crude oil starting in 1910. By the 1940s (when Trinidad supplied some 65% of the British Empire's oil production) it had become the main sector of the economy. British and American investment saw the establishment of new oil companies in Trinidad and later the discovery of large offshore deposits in the Gulf of Paria. In more recent years, the government of Trinidad and Tobago has been actively involved in the oil and gas industries, through nationalisation, investment and joint venture arrangements with foreign investors, though there has been significant divestment in the 1990s. As well as producing crude oil, the country is also an important regional refiner.

Although oil production was actually in decline at the beginning of the 1970s, the international oil crisis of 1973 and the subsequent rise in prices led to an increase in production and a period of rapid expansion in the national economy (1974-1982). During these years, the government used the country's abundance of natural gas (commercially exploited since the 1950s) to encourage diversification away from oil and the development of petrochemical, iron and steel industries. Trinidad and Tobago became an important producer of nitrogenous fertilizers, ammonia, urea and methanol, ranking as the world's second largest exporter of anhydrous ammonia (after the former USSR).

23

The fall in international oil prices in 1983 caused a prolonged period of decline in the Trinidad and Tobago economy, but there has been a return to growth in the 1990s, and the oil and natural gas sectors continue to be of major importance.

Agriculture in the colonies

Despite the occasional importance of minerals, for most of the last five centuries the economy of most Caribbean territories has been dominated by agriculture. At some times, and in some places, this has meant subsistence farming. Supplemented by fishing, this was the basis of the Amerindian economies. More recently, it has been important in modern Haiti, and in parts of Jamaica and the eastern Caribbean islands after the end of slavery, and the production of food for local consumption has always been a feature of most Caribbean societies to some extent. Nevertheless, Caribbean agriculture has generally meant the production of export crops for an extra-regional market.

The sugar-cane had been introduced into the Spanish settlements in the Canary Islands from the Mediterranean in the late 15th century, and it was from here that Columbus took cane plants to the Caribbean on his second voyage (1493). Within a few decades, sugar had been successfully established in Hispaniola, Cuba, Puerto Rico and Jamaica. The first record of the export of sugar from the Caribbean to Europe is in 1516, when six loaves of sugar were presented to the Emperor Charles V. They had been brought from Hispaniola, and it was this island where sugar at first achieved its greatest success. In 1530 a total of twelve ships arrived in Spain bringing perhaps more than a thousand tons of sugar. By this time, however, the Portuguese were developing a sugar industry in Brazil. This proved a formidable competitor, and by the late 16th century Caribbean sugar was in decline, and the Spanish found it more profitable to turn large areas of the Greater Antilles into cattle ranches, with meat and hides being exported to their mainland colonies.

When other European powers began to challenge the Spanish monopoly in the Caribbean in the early 17th century, their aims were partly strategic. The gold and silver which flowed from the Americas was seen as a major source of the power which Spain enjoyed in Europe, and settlements in the Caribbean might be used as bases for attacking the Spanish in the Americas and so furthering the aims of Spain's opponents in European conflicts. Caribbean colonies also had potential as a means of getting rid of what were seen as surplus population and undesirable elements, in much the same way as the British exploited Australia as a convict settlement in the late 18th and early 19th centuries. However – and apart from the

24

continuing chimaera of gold – it was hoped that wealth could be obtained from tropical produce. It was this which represented the main attraction for the proliferation of Caribbean colonies in the early 1600s – one well-fortified settlement would have been adequate for keeping up raids on Spanish territory.

In the early stages, colonists attempted a wide range of crops, with varying degrees of success. Tobacco, ginger, cotton and indigo were the most important, but a number of minor products also brought their rewards. From the 16th century until the end of the 18th, the resin of the lignum vitae tree was widely believed to offer a cure for syphilis, and as a result fetched high prices; later the hardness of the wood led to its being used for a number of special purposes, such as the sheaves of the pulley blocks used in naval rigging. Well into the 19th century, a favoured treatment in western medicine for almost any complaint was the administration of a laxative, and a preparation of aloes exported from Barbados was commonly used for this purpose. Later Aruba became an important producer, exporting 375,000 kilos in 1912; even in 1951, when synthetic products had reduced the demand for aloes, Aruba exported some 7,500 kilos, or about 30% of the world's production.

The early 17th-century settlements were in some ways abominably ill-organised. Settlers were dependent on unreliable imports of provisions from Europe, or on what they could supply themselves with. The early Barbadian settlers solved some of their problems by bringing in a group of Amerindians from the South American mainland. These and other Indians provided important expertise on production of local foodstuffs, helped to popularise the hammock, and contributed to the development of a local pottery industry (which was later to be of value to sugar production, since clay pots were used in the curing of sugar). Their reward was to be enslaved. We may also note that, just as Africans had early been introduced into the Spanish territories in the Caribbean, the same was true of the colonies of other European powers – there were ten Africans on the ship which brought the first settlers to Barbados in 1627.

However, for some years, the majority of the settlers were Europeans. In the early 17th century, political and economic conditions in much of Europe were unsettled – this is the period of the Thirty Years' War (1618-1648). England, for example, faced a severe economic depression in the 1620s as a result of the decline of the wool industry, with real wages near their lowest levels for the whole of the period from 1250 to 1950. The Caribbean might not be superficially attractive – it was a long way away, the hazards of the voyage and of tropical disease were very real, and clearing virgin land for cultivation was unquestionably hard work – but it offered the hope of riches to both gentleman adventurers with some capital to invest and indentured servants who could contribute only their labour, which they sold in advance for a period of years in exchange for their passage and keep, and the expectation of a lump sum and perhaps a piece of land at the end of it.

'Filthie Noveltie': tobacco in the Caribbean

The habit of tobacco smoking was introduced into England from Virginia in the 1580s, and although it was described as early as 1604 by King James I as 'A custome lothsome to the eye, hateful to the Nose, harmefull to the braine, dangerous to the Lungs, and in the blacke stinking fume thereof, neerest resembling the horrible Stigian smoke of the pit that is bottomelesse,' the 'filthie noveltie' was 'daily practised in this generall vse of *Tobacco* by all sorts and complexions of people.' The systematic cultivation of tobacco for export was established in Virginia about 1616, and in 1619 one writer in the New World said it fetched 3/6 a lb. and a grower could make £200 a year – this was at a time when a farm labourer averaged 4/- a week or about £10..8s a year (if he was so fortunate as to be able to work for the entire year). In the late 1620s, tobacco was highly profitable, and its production was one of the aims of early English settlement in the Caribbean. Sir Thomas Warner's first settlement in St. Kitts in 1624 consisted of less than two dozen men, and one tobacco crop was destroyed by a hurricane, but Warner still managed to return to England in 1625 with 9,500 pounds of tobacco, and this proved so profitable that the following year he was able to go back to St. Kitts with 400 recruits. Tobacco prices fell briefly in 1630, but then recovered sufficiently in the period 1631-1634 to encourage settlers to continue planting it in preference to other crops. After this, tobacco declined; Caribbean planters were unable to compete with those of Virginia in terms of either quality or price, and began to seek other crops. As early as 1630, Barbados was exporting cotton, but this was also subject to price fluctuations, with a high in the late 1630s soon followed by a decline. Ginger was also tried, but European demand proved to be inelastic, and increased production forced prices down.

Nevertheless, the early years of tobacco cultivation brought success to the new eastern Caribbean colonies. In 1639, there were more English settlers in Barbados than in Virginia, even though as late as 1647 at least one-third of the island was still uncultivated. A modern historian, R. C. Batie, has estimated that with land still comparatively easy to come by, it was possible to get started as a tobacco farmer in Barbados in the early years with an initial investment of only £2. The island was still a predominantly male frontier society, in which even the wealthier settlers lived in houses

Cigar factory, Cuba   *Philip Wolmuth*

little better than shacks, and heavy drinking was virtually the only recreation.
The so-called 'starving time' of 1630, and an epidemic, perhaps of yellow
fever, which killed thousands in 1647 contributed to a sense of
impermanence.   But by the later 1640s a number of circumstances were in
place which gave Barbados the opportunity to make a major change which
was to transform not only that island, but in due course much of the
Caribbean, both economically and socially.

The sugar revolution

Barbados benefited from its position as the most easterly of the Caribbean
islands and from the prevailing winds, which combined to make it a natural
first port of call for ships from Europe.   By this point it had a relatively
large population which provided both a labour force and a means of defence.
These factors enabled the island to benefit from external circumstances.
The Dutch had conquered a large area of north-eastern Brazil in 1630 and
developed European markets for the sugar produced there, but a Portuguese
revolt against Dutch rule in 1645 had disrupted sugar cultivation in Brazil,
which then produced about 80% of the world's sugar, and caused a sharp
increase in sugar prices in European markets, at the same time that tobacco
prices were declining and Caribbean planters were looking for new crops.
This coincided with the Civil Wars in the British Isles (1639-51), which
left the English colonists in the Caribbean largely free of effective control
from their home government.   It is not clear exactly when or from where

sugar was first introduced into Barbados, but it was at this point the Dutch, faced with the Portuguese revolt which finally drove them out of Brazil in 1654, were looking for both an alternative source of sugar and an alternative market for their slave trade. They had already been trading with Barbados from the 1630s. It is possible the Dutch helped the Barbadian planters with technical expertise they had acquired in Brazil; they certainly helped them by providing capital and selling them slaves on credit. In return, the Dutch for some years monopolised the trade of Barbados to their advantage and to that of the Barbadian planters who were able to sell their sugar at good prices.

In 1652 a fleet sent by the English parliament ended the virtual autonomy the Barbadians had enjoyed during the Civil War period. Thereafter the English government was able to enforce in the Caribbean a general (though far from complete) compliance with the Navigation Acts passed in 1651 and later years, which were intended to ensure that the production and commerce of English colonies benefited England and not the Netherlands or some other power. By then, the 'sugar revolution' was well established. While other crops persisted, the largest part of the Barbadian economy had come to depend on sugar, and there had been a change from a situation where comparatively small holdings were worked mainly by indentured servants from Europe to one where the main unit of production was a much larger plantation whose labour was supplied by slaves brought from Africa. The reasons for this, and some of its enduring consequences, are discussed below (Chapter 6). Sugar brought prosperity to the Barbadian planters, and by 1680 the island surpassed all the other English colonies in the Americas in both wealth and population.

This pre-eminence was not to last. The Barbadian example and methods of sugar production were imitated in other parts of the Caribbean. Settlers from Barbados helped to establish a successful English sugar colony in Suriname in the 1650s, but it was the Dutch who reaped the benefit when that territory was ceded to them in 1667. Jamaica, captured by the English from the Spanish in 1655, followed slowly, but had the advantage of a much larger area of mainly virgin land; by 1720 Jamaican production was overtaking that of Barbados. Even St. Kitts, much smaller than Barbados, was producing as much sugar by 1750, and Antigua nearly as much, in spite of the disadvantage of low rainfall.

An even greater rival developed in Hispaniola after 1697, when France gained the western third of the island; by the late 18th century the French colony of St.-Domingue had become the world's most important producer of both sugar and coffee. The Haitian Revolution (1791-1804) left the economy of the former colony in ruins, and it was Cuba, a comparatively

Interior of boiling house, Barbados, c.1920   *Courtesy of John Gilmore*

minor producer until the short-lived British conquest of Havana in 1762 brought about a massive influx of slave labour, which developed rapidly to become the region's major supplier of sugar in the 19th century.

By this time, other parts of the world had become significant producers of sugar. In 1747 a Prussian chemist called Andraeas Sigismond Marggraf published details of how sugar could be obtained from beet. Only at the beginning of the 19th century did another Prussian, Franz Carl Achard, undertake large-scale production of beet sugar, but the importance of this development was soon appreciated elsewhere. War between Britain and France was making imports of cane sugar into continental Europe exceedingly expensive, and from 1811 the Emperor Napoleon gave official encouragement to the manufacture of beet sugar. Even after the return of peace (1815) this continued, and the beet sugar industry developed in France and elsewhere, until eventually it was to be found across large areas of Europe and parts of North America. At first it was only a minor competitor to cane sugar: in 1839 cane still represented more than 95% of world sugar production. But in 1881 this figure fell below 50% for the first time.

During the 19th century, cane sugar production was begun or greatly increased in many places, including Mauritius, Java, Australia, Fiji, Hawaii, Louisiana and other parts of the United States. As a result, overall production increased dramatically and the Caribbean, from being the world's major supplier, was reduced to the position of being only one competitor among many. At the same time, prices for most of the 19th century were generally much lower than they had been in the period from 1750-1820.

The history of sugar is the classic example of how Caribbean producers have nearly always been dependent on factors over which they have had little or no control. In the 18th century, colonial lobbies in Britain and France were able to secure protected markets for their sugar and 'as rich as a West India planter' became a proverbial expression. The planters in the colonies paid a price, however, in restrictions on where they could sell their produce and where they could obtain their supplies (including the slaves who provided their essential labour force), and these restrictions were meant to benefit the mother country rather than the colonies. Manufacturing in the colonies was actively discouraged so that everything which was wanted would be imported from the mother country or, as second best, from another colony of the same power. Caribbean mills and boiling houses turned canes into sugar, but the sugar was exported as a raw material which was refined in Europe before it was sold to the consumer. This system, known as mercantilism, ensured that while the Caribbean produced the sugar, much of the wealth generated by this process ended up outside the region. Formally, mercantilism disappeared with the 19th-century enthusiasm for free trade, but as far as the Caribbean is concerned it set a pattern which has continued to the present.

If sugar brought wealth to a lucky few, that wealth could be easily lost. War brought high prices, but also increased risks. A planter could be ruined if a hurricane or a slave rebellion destroyed his crop.

Social and political change in Britain which led to parliamentary reform in 1832 put an end to the influence of the West Indian lobby. The abolition of slavery (1834-38) deprived the planter of his guaranteed source of cheap labour; soon afterwards Parliament bowed to the prevailing economic wisdom in favour of free trade and abolished the protection which the British colonial producer of sugar had enjoyed since the 17th century. Import duties on sugar were gradually reduced, and by 1854 all distinction between sugar from British colonies and sugar from elsewhere was abolished. In some parts of the Caribbean, this spelt ruin for the sugar industry – not necessarily an unmitigated disaster, as the ex-slaves and other small proprietors sometimes benefited from increased access to land as a result of the planters' discomfiture. There was a dramatic decline in production in Jamaica after Emancipation, while in some of the smaller islands exports had dwindled almost to vanishing or ceased altogether by the end of the 19th century. Sugar survived and actually expanded in Trinidad and British Guiana because the introduction of indentured labourers from India provided a new cheap workforce; in some of the smaller territories such as Barbados, Antigua and St. Kitts, the planters kept going because the density of population enabled them to keep wages low.

There have been occasional periods of prosperity for the sugar islands since. The First World War turned much of western Europe's beet-producing areas into battlefields. For a few years the Caribbean producer enjoyed a boom in sugar prices so great that it was known in Cuba as the 'Dance of the Millions', but, as so often happens, the boom was followed by a collapse. The average c.i.f. (cost, insurance, freight) price of raw sugar on the London market in 1921 was less than a third of what it had been the previous year, and the price fell further in the succeeding years. Since the late 19th century, sugar has been produced in the Caribbean with steadily increasing efficiency: scientific plant breeding offers varieties which give more cane to the same area of land, while improved factories get more juice out of the same amount of cane, and more sugar out of the same amount of juice.

This has seldom been enough to ensure the viability of the industry, which has generally depended for its survival on special arrangements which are more dependent on political than on economic considerations. Examples include the system of 'imperial preference' which Britain introduced in 1919, abandoning its previous support for free trade in order to tax imports of 'empire-grown' sugar at a lower rate than those from foreign countries, and its successor, the Commonwealth Sugar Agreement (1951-1974), which gave Caribbean (and other Commonwealth) sugar producers quotas for import into Britain at negotiated prices. This has in turn been replaced by agreements, not with Britain, but with the European Community under protocols to the Lomé Conventions.

The future of these protocols is in doubt. Exports of sugar from the Caribbean to the United States are regulated by quota, but Caribbean countries have little influence over the setting of these quotas, which were significantly reduced in the late 1980s in response to domestic lobbying by US sugar interests. For many years Cuba benefited from its relationship with the Soviet Union, which enabled it to exchange sugar for oil and other essential supplies, but the collapse of the Soviet Union ended this system and caused a profound economic crisis in Cuba.

Diversification

Other crops were introduced or developed in the 19th century as alternatives to sugar. Nutmeg was tried in several parts of the region and proved to be particularly successful in Grenada, which is now (with Indonesia) one of the world's largest producers, as well as exporting other spices. St. Vincent arrowroot – largely a crop of peasant proprietors – was used to produce an edible starch which became a staple of Victorian kitchens and sick-rooms, and found a new market in the 1990s as a filler for some types of computer papers.

Coffee had been grown in the region since the 18th century, and continues to be a major or significant export from Jamaica, Cuba, Haiti and the Dominican Republic. An excellent product and skilful marketing have combined to make Jamaica's Blue Mountain coffee the most expensive in the world. Cocoa production became important in the Windward Islands and Trinidad. At the beginning of the 20th century Trinidad was the third largest producer of cocoa in the world (after Ecuador and Brazil), but the industry was virtually wiped out, first by witchbroom disease and then by increased competition from West African sources. For some decades limes seemed promising in several islands, but by the 1920s limes fell victim to withertip disease and to the development of cheaper sources for citric acid.

The export of bananas from the region began in the 1860s when American ships' captains started to take bananas from Cuba and Jamaica to the USA. Jamaica enjoyed something of a banana boom from the late 1870s until the 1920s, when the crop was virtually wiped out by disease. The industry has survived lean years and bananas are still Jamaica's second crop, after sugar. After the failure of limes and cocoa, the Windward Islands turned to bananas, which have become vital to the economies of Dominica, St. Lucia, St. Vincent and, to a lesser extent, Grenada. Bananas are extremely vulnerable to hurricane damage, and islands have several times seen entire crops wiped out overnight. Caribbean bananas are also unable to compete in terms of price with those produced by US-owned multinationals in Latin America (though claims are made for their superior flavour) and they have for many years depended on protected markets in Europe. US insistence that this amounts to unfair trade practices means that this protection is unlikely to last much longer.

Persistent problems with traditional exports have long led Caribbean entrepreneurs and governments to seek alternative sources of income in manufacturing and service industries of various kinds. Of these, the oldest and most successful is tourism.

Bananas: free trade or fair trade?

Although there were earlier efforts in the 1930s, the banana industry in the Windward Islands (Dominica, St. Lucia, St. Vincent and Grenada) did not become important until after the Second World War, when the British government actively encouraged it as a source of fruit from within the sterling area, as opposed to 'dollar bananas' from US-owned multinationals.

Production expanded rapidly, and although there have been repeated crises in the industry, it remains of vital importance to the countries concerned. In the Windwards as a whole in 1992, bananas accounted for

53.5% of domestic exports, and banana exports for 15.1% of GDP. Production is labour-intensive, based on small, family-owned and operated farms of only a few acres, and some 15,000 farmers and their families in the Windwards are directly dependent on bananas. As the prime minister of Dominica, Edison James, told a meeting of the World Trade Organisation in 1998:

> The industry [in the Windward Islands] is the major source of employment, and the majority of households receive an income, directly or indirectly from the production and marketing of bananas. It is a rural industry in which almost the entire rural community is engaged, producing bananas on predominantly small family plots, often situated on hill-sides. A substantial number of the banana farmers are women. At the moment, there is no system more guaranteed to ensure that a cash income reaches the neediest in the society or to address the special problems of the rural poor. In addition to its contribution to economic development the banana industry is, therefore, a significant guarantor of social and political stability not only in my own banana producing country but in the entire Caribbean region [...] In a small island economy the development options are not many. The reform process is painful and the diversification process difficult.

Unfortunately, the production costs of Windwards bananas are comparatively high, and consistent quality is difficult to achieve: the varieties grown and problems of internal transportation caused by the terrain make it hard to avoid bruising, for example. By contrast, Latin American growers enjoy higher yields from large plantations on flat land worked by employees at wage rates significantly below those in the Caribbean. The 1989 report of the Windward Islands Banana Growers' Association (WINBAN) claimed production in the Windwards averaged six tons an acre, compared to sixteen tons an acre for most of Latin America. A 1987 WINBAN study showed wage rates in the Windwards to be three times higher than in Colombia. Windwards producers also faced the threat of their crops being destroyed by hurricanes, which seldom affected Latin American producers, at least until Hurricane Mitch struck the banana-producing areas of Honduras in 1998.

As a result, Windwards banana producers depended on the continuance of preferential trading regimes, and Britain managed to secure this when it joined the European Community in 1973. The Banana Protocol to the 1975 Lomé Convention between the EC and the African, Caribbean and

Banana carriers, Jamaica, c.1905   *Courtesy of John Gilmore*

Pacific (ACP) countries also continued special arrangements for the former colonies or overseas territories of Britain, France and a number of other EC member states, while other EC countries imported dollar bananas. The introduction of the Single European Market in 1992 led to prolonged negotiations and the eventual adoption by the European Union of a new banana regime which was to come into effect on 1 July 1993 and remain in force until 2002. This was a compromise which secured some degree of continued protection for bananas from ACP countries and also from overseas territories of EU members (including Martinique and Guadeloupe).

However, most dollar bananas are exported by three US-based international companies – Chiquita (the successor to the pioneering United Fruit Company), Del Monte, and Dole – which have enormous lobbying power. In 1992 Latin American fruit accounted for 75% of world-wide exports in an international banana trade worth US$7 billion; the Windwards' share, by contrast, was 2.6%. Dollar bananas accounted for 62% of EU imports (with Chiquita, Del Monte and Dole supplying over 40%), while 20% came from overseas territories of EU members and 18% from ACP countries.

Nevertheless, in the 1990s the US and some Latin American countries made a series of official complaints to the World Trade Organisation, claiming that the EU's banana import regime breached international agreements on free trade. By 1999, the US was threatening punitive measures against a range of EU exports to the US (all totally unrelated to bananas). An editorial in the *Financial Times* (5 March 1999) described it as 'The US government [...] responding to the massive lobbying power of one company – Chiquita – which seeks to dominate Central American banana production and the lucrative transatlantic trade.' While the *FT* noted that the EU was not without blame in the dispute, and claimed that the EU import regime benefited banana traders rather than the producers, many in the Caribbean view the actions of the US as an unwarranted attack on the region. St. Lucia's foreign minister, George Odlum, was quoted in August 1999 as saying that Caribbean leaders 'feel sore, that America who has been a traditional friend for many decades, has now decided to take so tough a line against those small vulnerable countries.'

Others noted the far-reaching implications of the banana dispute, and claimed it demonstrated that might was right in international trade. 'Free trade does not mean fair trade,' said an editorial in the Barbados *Nation* (29 August 1999):

> [...] when we talk of bananas we would be wise to remember that the special regime for bananas exists for the same reason as the special regimes for sugar and rice. The assault on the banana regime is only the starting point [...]
>
> The same countries that crusade against a few trade preferences that benefit a few small island economies operate the most heavily subsidised agricultural economies in the world and have the gall to quarrel when Jamaica seeks to protect its market from a flood of cheap chicken from outside. They can do this because they made the WTO rules that allow them to keep their agricultural subsidies.
>
> The subsidies which the high and mighty have thereby entrenched afford greater protection to the United States and the European Union agriculture than the system of preferences could ever offer small Caribbean economies.

New marketing strategies, such as the development of niche markets and a trend towards making a change to organic production, offer some hope to Caribbean banana producers. However, whether they will be able to survive in the long term remains uncertain.

3. The tourist crop

Hospitality and a Genteel behav[iour] is shown to every gentelman stranger by the gentelman Inhab[itants.] Taverns they have none but in their Towns so that Travellers is oblig'd to go to private houses however the Island being but ab[ou]t 22 Miles in length & 14 in width prevents their being much infested with [the]m.

From George Washington's diary of his visit to Barbados, 1751.

There is one other crop which I am glad to see coming in now, at long last, for attention. I mean the tourist crop [...] This is one of the most paying crops for any colony. In the Bahamas and Bermuda the tourist crop has practically abolished the Colonial Debt, and in Jamaica, they bring in a handsome sum annually to the general revenue. Why should we not have tourists here?

Sir Norman Lamont, speaking to the Naparima Agricultural Society, Trinidad, 17 November 1931.

The time is now ripe for us in the Caribbean to open our eyes and wake up to the real world, and to realize that we cannot leave the unfolding of our destiny to the whims of powerful media-houses and public-relations agencies, some of which have introduced the fantasia of reggae-music, dreadlocks, and ganja. The world of happy natives, swaying to the rhythms of calypso-music has, in fact, come back to haunt us. It was created by outside interests, and is, therefore, still acceptable to them. If we could stay frozen in that world, forever singing, forever carrying bananas to the docks at twilight, we would probably not upset the paradisiacal image. At the same time, we would also deprive visitors and ourselves of the joy of discovering the real Caribbean.

Olive Lewin, 'Banana Boat Song Forever?', in *Come Mek Me Hol' Yu' Han': The Impact of Tourism on Traditional Music* (Jamaica Memory Bank, 1986)

From 'fatal climate' to health resort

In the middle of the 19th century a cholera epidemic swept through many Caribbean islands. It reached Barbados in 1854, and between May and August it killed perhaps as many as 20,000 people, or about as much as one-fifth of the entire population. The worst disaster in the island's history, it nevertheless, in the opinion of the Rev. James Young Edghill, a local Moravian clergyman who lived through it, brought unexpected benefits: 'The poverty that prevailed was revealed. In many a house there was neither glass nor spoon to administer medicine. Men and women lay upon bare boards awaiting death [...] It taught the have-somethings that they owed a duty to the have-nothings, for it showed that disease may begin in the cabin, but it will spread to the castle if there is not the care of the latter for the former.' As a result, some of the filth was removed from Bridgetown, the city acquired a piped-water supply in 1861 (from 1886 extended to the country districts, where the public stand-pipes used to be known as 'Queen Victoria pumps'), and a rudimentary public health service came into being. While the island had once been known for its 'fatal climate', by 1886 the Rev. J. H. Sutton Moxly, author of *A West-Indian Sanatorium and a Guide to Barbados* was claiming that it was 'one of the most salubrious places in the world,' so much so that antiseptics were not used in surgery at the General Hospital in Bridgetown, as the air was too pure to require it.

More or less the same thing happened all over the region. It is true that even a century or so earlier there were occasional visitors who came to the Caribbean of their own accord and for a reason other than the hope of making money. The best known example is a young Virginian called George Washington, who stayed in Barbados for nearly seven weeks in 1751, accompanying his brother Lawrence, who was suffering from tuberculosis and who had been told a stay in a warmer climate would be good for him. In his diary, George Washington warmly praised Barbadian hospitality, and he seems to have had a most enjoyable time, at least until he caught smallpox and had to be nursed back to health by a local doctor. The immunity which he thus acquired to a further attack of the disease was to stand him in good stead during a smallpox epidemic at a crucial point of the American War of Independence.

In general, however, the Caribbean shared with West Africa a reputation as the white man's grave – a reputation which was easily justified by statistics. Of the many thousands of European soldiers and sailors sent to the region in the course of the numerous conflicts up to the end of the Napoleonic wars (1815), far more died from disease than from enemy action. Overcrowded, ill-ventilated ships and barracks, appalling food, and a total

Healthy sea breezes of Barbados' east coast were a
major tourist attraction, c.1910

Courtesy of John Gilmore

absence of what would now be considered the most elementary sanitary
precautions all made their contributions, but these things were taken for
granted until well into the 19th century.   As late as 1840, for example,
67% of the garrison in Georgetown, British Guiana, died in an outbreak of
yellow fever. Gradually a better understanding of the causes of tropical
diseases developed, with an important stage being the suggestion made in
1881 by the Cuban doctor, Carlos Finlay, that mosquitos were involved in
the transmission of yellow fever.

In the early 20th century, somewhat authoritarian measures adopted
first in Havana and then in the Panama Canal Zone by US military
authorities under the supervision of Col. W. C. Gorgas demonstrated
conclusively that control of mosquitos meant control of both yellow fever
and malaria.   The sanitary inspector with his cork hat (pith helmet) and
his little metal ladle for dipping into any standing accumulation of water
in the search for mosquito larvae became a familiar figure in island after
island and the two great scourges disappeared almost entirely.

The promotion of Jamaica as a health resort had begun even earlier,
not long after the cholera epidemic which caused enormous loss of life in
that island in 1851, and before there was any real improvement in public
health to speak of. This may have been a deliberate attempt to use tourism
as a means of encouraging North American investment in the island in the
period of economic depression which followed the end of slavery and

preferential sugar duties. By the 1890s, what had been known as the Hellshire Hills because of their nearness to malarial swamps had been renamed the Healthshire Hills. Statistics are hard to come by for the early period, and numbers were certainly tiny by later standards – one contemporary estimate placed total visitor arrivals for Jamaica in 1906 at 7,000 – but by the beginning of the 20th century the tourist in a recognisably modern sense had become an established feature of the Caribbean.

The hotel boom

With the tourist came a transformation in the region's hotels. From the late 18th century, if not earlier, there were hotels and lodging houses to be found in virtually every town in the Caribbean. They were places locals and visitors went to drink, and at least sometimes they doubled as brothels, but they did provide accommodation for what would now be called business travellers, of whom there were usually enough to provide a moderate income for a small hotel run by an owner-manager. Until at least the middle of the 19th century, it was often the case that, as one business traveller, the post office functionary and novelist Anthony Trollope, put it, perhaps with some exaggeration:

> There is a mystery about hotels in the British West Indies. They are always kept by fat, middle-aged coloured ladies, who have no husbands [...] These ladies are generally called Miss So-and-So; Miss Jenny This, or Miss Jessy That; but they invariably seemed to have a knowledge of the world, especially of the male hotel-frequenting world, hardly compatible with a retiring maiden state of life.

By the end of the century, Miss Jenny and Miss Jessy had given way to a new type of establishment, symbolised by the Marine Hotel in Barbados, begun in 1878 and replaced a decade later with a much larger structure boasting 200 rooms. The owner-manager of 'the Marine' for many years in its early period, a man who gets an obligatory mention in any survey of the history of tourism in Barbados, was an American, G. S. Pomeroy. The Titchfield Hotel in Port Antonio on Jamaica's north coast was started by Captain Lorenzo Dow Baker, one of the pioneers of the banana trade and of what became the United Fruit Company. A skilled practitioner of 'vertical integration' long before the concept was named, the company controlled the purchase and marketing of a large share of Jamaican banana production, owned the ships which transported them to North America, and carried tourists in both directions, as well as owning the hotel in which many of

Tourist hotel, c.1910   *Courtesy of John Gilmore*

them would stay. An enduring feature of the industry, that of government involvement, goes back at least to 1860, when the Royal Victoria Hotel in Nassau was built by the Bahamian government.

In the aftermath of 'the Cholera' (as the mid-19th century epidemic was long called), and with the reduction of the more ferocious tropical diseases, there was an emphasis on the idea of the Caribbean as a health resort. At first it was not the beaches, but the mountainous interior of Jamaica (safely distant from the fever-bearing miasma of the coastal towns) that was advertised as an attraction, and many visitors to Barbados stayed on the east coast, drawn by the vigorous and supposedly health-giving Atlantic breezes, rather than by the sea-bathing which was here (unlike the much more placid west coast) often too rough to be safely indulged in. The simple pleasure of exchanging winter at home for a warm climate abroad proved to be a major and enduring part of the Caribbean's appeal – and there was the important fact that the northern winter coincided with the drier season in the Caribbean; since mosquitos need water in which to breed, it was a healthier time of year for visitors and locals alike. By the beginning of the 20th century, however, there was less emphasis on the health aspect, and a more purely recreational approach to tourism was usual. For the 1906-7 tourist season, for example, the Titchfield advertised itself as:

The Largest and Finest Resort Hotel in the West Indies. American Plan. Location Unsurpassed in the World. Facilities for Riding,

41

Driving, Automobiling, Boating, Fishing, Tennis, and all Outdoor Sports and Recreations. Sea Bathing Un[e]qualled anywhere.

There have been changes of emphasis – there is no specific mention of golf, now an apparently indispensable feature of a successful tourist destination, though golf was certainly available to pre-1914 visitors to a number of Caribbean destinations, including Jamaica – but this is not very different from the usual tourist product offered today. Changes in transportation and in the economies of tourist-sending countries have, however, enormously changed both the volume of the trade and its importance to the Caribbean.

In 1914, the journey by ship from England to the Caribbean took about two weeks or a little less, while from New York to Nassau or Havana was four days, and to Kingston, Jamaica, about six days. Fares varied considerably, but the United Fruit Company offered a first-class return from New York to Kingston for $85.50, while the Royal Mail Steam Packet Company offered a first-class return from Southampton to Barbados for £38. These fares included all meals, and may seem incredibly cheap by modern standards, but it is worth comparing the fact that a good wage for a cook or a maid in the Caribbean at the same time was £20 or $96 a year, while an agricultural labourer would be lucky to get a shilling (24¢) a day. The cost of the journey, and the time it took, meant that early 20th-century tourists were generally rich, and that they were often in no need of hurrying back to the demands of a job. Some simply treated the return trip in much the same way as a modern cruise passenger, and only disembarked for shore excursions, but those who did stay at any one island might do so for much longer than would normally be the case now: a matter of weeks or even months, rather than days.

The development of cheap and reliable air transport from the 1950s onwards has altered this pattern dramatically. New York to Jamaica is now less than four hours, while some Caribbean destinations can be reached from Britain in eight or nine hours – half that if you are flying Concorde to Barbados. The cost of fares in real terms is much less than it was at the beginning of the century, while at the same time the disposable income of a large part of the population of North America and Europe has risen significantly. Tourism in the Caribbean, as in other parts of the world, has become an industry dependent on moving large numbers of people. In 1952, Barbados saw 5,415 arrivals by sea, with another 15,510 by air. By 1997, this figure had risen to a total of 472,290 visitors, a record figure which does not include cruise-ship passengers. Sutton Moxly could claim in 1886 that 'With Barbados [...] there is no question of life or death [...]

Cuban nightclub, c.1940s

Courtesy of John Gilmore

whether Englishmen come or stay,' but with the decline of traditional exports and the uncertain future of long-established markets virtually every Caribbean economy has become increasingly dependent on tourism. At the same time, while the traditional winter 'tourist season' continues to be a peak period, summer arrivals have increased enormously, and most destinations now rely on attracting visitors the whole year round.

A new form of mercantilism

While it may be difficult to see any alternative, tourism has problems of its own. Air travel has not only shortened journey times, it has also encouraged the growth of shorter holidays. A two-week, or even one-week trip to the Caribbean is now both feasible and normal for many North Americans and Europeans, but while this has encouraged the growth of visitor numbers, it means that many visitors are budget conscious – they not only spend less on their visit as a whole, but they spend less per day than visitors of an earlier generation. But at the same time, they represent greatly increased demands on the often limited infrastructure of small islands and have a greater impact on host societies.

To use the earlier example, in 1952 the annual numbers of visitors to Barbados were equivalent to about 10% of the resident population, while in 1997 they were nearly 200%. The problems this causes in terms of additional demands placed on water supplies and sewage systems are easily imagined. The basic demand for an increased number of hotel rooms has

43

Table 2: Tourist Arrivals, 1987 and 1996 (millions) by country, and country of origin in 1997

Country	Pop (1999)	1987 arrivals	1996 arrivals	From US (1997)	From Canada (1997)	From Europe (1997)
Antigua & Barbuda	64,246	177,000	228,200	64,689	18,580	80,933
Bahamas	283,759	1,479,900	1,633,100	1,056,990	66,740	99,865
Barbados	259,751	421,900	447,100	108,095	58,824	220,460
Belize	235,789	99,300	349,100	-	-	-
Dominica	64,881	26,700	63,300	13,378	1,592	10,862
Dominican Republic	8,129,734	911,300	1,925,600	326,299	128,991	754,090
Grenada	97,008	57,400	108,200	26,991	4,335	34,009
Guyana	705,156	59,800	91,900	28,989	10,268	4,778
Haiti	6,884,264	121,800	150,100	-	-	-
Jamaica	2,652,443	738,800	1,162,400	802,808	99,216	210,632
St.Kitts & Nevis	42,838	64,600	84,200	33,081	6,738	11,880
St. Lucia	154,020	111,600	235,700	73,446	16,043	96,393
St Vincent & Grenadines	120,519	46,000	57,900	17,170	4,071	16,234
Suriname	431,156	27,000	53,300	-	-	-
Trinidad & Tobago	1,102,096	201,700	265,900	91,259	29,694	55,057

Source: OAS

led to building on a scale which has had a serious impact on many islands. Some recent entrants into the mass tourism market have to some extent learnt from the mistakes of others and endeavoured to plan their industry accordingly – Aruba, for example, has based its industry (which has expanded enormously since the mid-1980s) around a comparatively small number of large hotels in one area, leaving most of the rest of the island untouched. In other cases, there has been little control until recent times. A century of development, the pace of which increased considerably from the 1950s, has left Barbados with an almost continuous line of hotels, guest-houses and tourism-related businesses along its south and west coasts.

The basic outlines of the industry, however, have not changed greatly since the early 20th century. The small, locally-owned hotel or guest-house has never disappeared entirely, and there have been some successful large-scale developments by Caribbean entrepreneurs, of which the best known examples are Butch Stewart's Sandals and John Issa's SuperClubs (both Jamaican). However, many of the larger hotels are owned or managed by foreign interests, often multinational corporations with the resources to market their Caribbean destinations as part of a wide-ranging tourism product. This is often something which has been actively encouraged by Caribbean governments which have seen foreign investment as a means of bringing money into the country and of developing tourism rapidly when an alternative was needed to traditional sources of revenue. Generous tax holidays and other concessions have frequently been part of the package. Direct government ownership of hotels, popular in the aftermath of independence, has declined as many such hotels have been privatised.

One result is that the tourist industry often seems like a new form of mercantilism. The Caribbean produces the product, indeed *is* the product, but a large part of the profits to be made from selling holidays in the Caribbean goes to airlines, cruise ship companies, tour operators and international hotel chains owned by outsiders. Local governments do receive revenue from the industry in the form of taxation, and local communities benefit from the provision of employment, but this has to be balanced against the fact that in return the industry demands the provision of facilities (such as improved roads and airports) for which governments have to pay, and that most of the employment is at a menial and low-paid level. It is also often seasonal or irregular, with hotels laying off workers in periods of low occupancy.

Hoteliers often appear to act as though the tourist, as customer, is always right, and governments are persuaded to accept the consequences of a policy of giving the tourist what he or she wants, or is believed to want. In the economic sphere, this means that a large part of what the industry consumes is imported. Some islands are much better than others at promoting their own cuisine, and ackee and salt-fish is often served to tourists in Jamaica, but few seem to find it strange that tourists in Curaçao get Dutch cheese for breakfast and 'Friesian Flag' milk for their coffee, or that hotels in Barbados have been known to run promotions for US beef, even though excellent local beef is available.

The same applies to the hotels themselves and their fittings. A large hotel in the Caribbean can look much like any other large hotel in the Caribbean (or anywhere else with a warm climate). The building itself may be made from locally produced cement blocks, and is perhaps painted with locally produced paint, but inside the tiles come from Italy, the bathroom fittings from Brazil and the bed sheets from the United States. The pictures on the walls of tropical vegetation or generically Caribbean scenes may well have come from a different island where such things are mass produced and cheaply available, rather than being bought from local artists – few visitors will either know or care. Very few hotels are built to take advantage of prevailing winds, and so each room will require an air-conditioning unit, probably American made. There will of course be a TV set, imported from Japan, or perhaps assembled in the region from imported components. Even the shell jewellery sold by the vendors on the beach outside will have been imported in bulk from the Philippines rather than locally made. In hotel boutiques and the tourist-oriented shops in local city-centres, imported goods greatly outnumber locally produced items in both bulk and value. The duty-free shopping which is a major attraction for visitors to Nassau, St. Maarten, Margarita or virtually any Caribbean destination depends on imported luxury items like perfume, china and crystal, not on locally produced souvenirs or works of art. To get visitors to come to the Caribbean, the region must spend large amounts of foreign exchange, local economic development is distorted, and dependence on the outside world is increased.

Tourism development sooner or later affects everybody in an island society. When demand from hotels has caused local lobster to disappear from over-fishing, the hotels will replace it with imported frozen lobster which local consumers cannot afford. Because they buy in bulk, hotels are often favoured customers where local producers are concerned, even in times of shortage – the local housewife may find that there is not an onion or a tomato or a pound of chicken wings to be had at the supermarket, but the tourist must not suffer. The price of land goes up, not just for beach-front property, but everywhere, and the local who finds that he cannot afford a view of the sea or that what used to be cheap agricultural land has been turned into a golf-course development with million-dollar villas sold to foreigners is unlikely to be happy about it. While some local people benefit from tourism, others feel excluded from the benefits. Issues like access to beaches, or heavy-handed security at hotels, are emotive ones, and it is easier to feel that the entire country has been sold to tourists and foreign developers than to discern whether there is any genuine benefit to the national economy as a whole.

All-exclusive: racism and tourism

The situation is not helped by another legacy of the past: in most of the Caribbean, nearly all tourists are white, while nearly all workers in the tourist industry, and most locals in general, are not. Sugar and slavery had left a legacy of racism and discrimination (see Chapter 6) and colonial officials and predominantly white local upper classes allowed some of the hotels developed in the early 20th century to operate formal colour bars. Officially, this will have disappeared in the 1950s or 1960s, usually with the approach of self-government or independence, but many Caribbean people can remember when this or that hotel or restaurant refused to let black people through the door except to cook or clean or wait at table, or, occasionally, as musicians and entertainers. It is not a happy memory, and it has some unfortunate consequences.

While a few islands like Aruba, Curaçao and Margarita are successful in attracting significant numbers of visitors from South America because of their proximity to the continent, there is a widespread assumption that tourists come from the north and that tourists are white. In most of the English-speaking Caribbean, very little effort is made to attract visitors from Latin America, or from among the black community in the United States and Canada, even though many Afro-Americans have family connections with the region. Apart from the fact that this is ignoring a potentially lucrative market, it helps to perpetuate a dangerous misconception. In at least some tourist destinations, many people will have heard of incidents where a black guest in a hotel – whether an Afro-American tourist or a local person attending some function – has been made to feel insulted because a member of staff has jumped to the conclusion that because they were not white they must be an undesirable intruder. It does not help that the member of staff involved is usually black themselves. Local opinion is understandably very sensitive about such incidents, or about ones where night clubs or similar businesses catering mainly for tourists appear to be attempting to operate some form of racial or perhaps class discrimination against local patrons under the guise of a dress code or a members-only policy.

Security guard, St. Lucia   *Philip Wolmuth*

The rapid spread of the all-inclusive concept since the 1980s has added to the problem. The all-inclusive takes a step further the 'American plan' popular in Caribbean hotels of the early 20th century, where the price of the room also included all meals. 'All inclusive' means just that: tourists pay in advance for a package which includes not only their rooms and all meals, but also drinks, entertainment, a wide range of recreational activities available on site, transport to and from the airport, and service charges. There may be sight-seeing trips included as well, but in general visitors see little need to stray outside the hotel grounds. The concept is understandably popular with visitors, who do not have to worry about a budget and need to spend very little once they have arrived in the Caribbean.

All-inclusive hotels make money because they operate at high occupancy rates and benefit from a law of averages: the guest who sets out to get more than his money's worth and pigs out at the buffet table and swills as much free booze as he can possibly manage the first couple of days will be too exhausted and hung over to keep it up for the rest of his stay. The security aspect is also an important factor from the hotel's point of view: with guests safely corralled on the premises under the watchful eyes of the hotel's own security staff for most of their stay, the possibility of unfortunate incidents arising out of unprogrammed contact with locals is reduced to a minimum.

Most tourists who choose an all-inclusive probably do not mind at all – they are looking for a sea, sun and sand vacation rather than for any profound insight into local culture. But things look rather different from the

48

perspective of the local citizen. In the Caribbean, just like in other parts of the world, many people like to go out for a drink or a meal. The all-inclusive is not designed to cope with people who are not resident guests – you cannot simply walk in off the street and buy a beer in the hotel bar or order a steak sandwich in the restaurant the way you could expect to do in an ordinary hotel. You have to buy a pass which, because it is usually intended to cover access to all the hotel's facilities for a minimum of several hours, will seem disproportionately expensive. However much the management may talk about being part of the community, a new all-inclusive will inevitably look as though it is designed to keep local people out. If an existing hotel decides to go all-inclusive, the impression is even worse. Local customers who might have used the facilities for a regular business lunch or an occasional celebration will now feel they are no longer welcome.

Even those involved in the tourist industry often feel that, unless you are directly employed by one, all-inclusives are bad news. Guests at an all-inclusive have already paid for their meals and accordingly have a good reason to eat their meals in their own hotel rather than dine out. If the hotel does have some sort of 'dine-around' arrangement, it will most probably be organised as part of a reciprocal arrangement with another hotel (perhaps even one owned or managed by the same group). This means less trade for restaurants which are not part of a hotel, and less trade for taxi-drivers. Local transport – to and from the airport, and for excursions – is one of the things which is 'included'; the hotel may have its own buses, driven by employees, or have a contract with one of the larger local firms. In either case, the 'small man' who owns and operates a single taxi is left out. Guests who spend all their time in the hotel do not go out to buy souvenirs or duty-free items as there are shops on the premises. This affects local businesses at all levels from the city-centre department store (which may feel obliged to accept an offer to rent space inside the hotel), to the beach vendor, who may be chased away from potential customers by the hotel's security guards, or allowed to operate only under strict conditions. All this adds up to a situation in which the all-inclusive is frequently seen as exclusive, in the worst possible sense of the word.

Big spenders?

The problems of land-based tourism are magnified where cruise-ships are concerned. The Caribbean cruise has been around since the late 19th century, but it has become a major industry in the last twenty years. There are more ships, bigger ships, and more passengers. Cruise-ship visitors are now to be counted in millions, rather than thousands, and for many destinations there are more of them each year than guests occupying hotel rooms. Like hotels on shore, cruise ship companies sell the Caribbean as a product, and in return expect the product to be of the highest possible standard.

In order to attract cruise visits, Caribbean governments spend millions on improving and expanding port facilities. They are also expected to provide other kinds of infrastructure, ranging from crime-free city centres to the supply of large quantities of water fit to drink and the capacity to dispose of large quantities of garbage. In return, all they receive is a small tax per passenger, which they cannot raise without the agreement of the cruise lines, who can simply threaten to take their ships elsewhere – attempts to get Caribbean governments to act together on the level of passenger tax have so far been a dismal failure.

The ships which cruise the Caribbean employ few Caribbean people and buy only a limited range and quantity of goods and services from Caribbean suppliers. Their operating costs are much lower than the land-based hotels with which they are in direct competition: they do not, for example, have to pay property taxes or corporation taxes to local governments. The cruise lines publish statistics to show that their passengers do spend significant amounts on shore visits, but these figures have been contested. By choosing who they recommend to their passengers, cruise lines also have the power to favour some shore businesses over others, whether these be duty-free stores or providers of sight-seeing tours and water-sports facilities. At the same time they compete with shore businesses in more than the provision of accommodation. Like guests at an all-inclusive hotel, cruise-ship passengers have little incentive to eat elsewhere. More and more shopping is now available on board – duty-free of course – so that passengers are encouraged to buy on the ship rather than on shore, which means increased profits for the cruise-line at the expense of local businesses.

The cruise lines claim that they provide a valuable service to the region in giving their passengers a sample of Caribbean destinations to which some of them will later return as land-based guests for a longer period than the few hours they have spent in any port. This argument has some validity, but it must be set against the industry's increasing tendency to promote the cruising experience itself, rather than the destinations visited, so that the ship itself becomes the destination.

Welcome to paradise: stereotypes of the Caribbean

The tourist industry as a whole is also vulnerable to outside factors. Cuba was a major destination for US visitors until the United States government imposed the still-extant trade embargo on the island in 1961 as a response

Cruise ships tower over St John's, capital of Antigua   *John Gilmore*

to Fidel Castro's Revolution; gradually Cuba built up alternative markets in Canada and Europe. Any unpleasant incident, however rare, whether it is something like an outbreak of food poisoning at a particular hotel, or a group of visitors on a sight-seeing bus getting robbed at gun-point, is likely to be widely reported in tourist-sending countries. Cancelled bookings affecting the entire industry in the country involved are the result. Sometimes Caribbean people feel that outsiders over-react to such things: cases of violent crime against visitors are extremely rare and the Caribbean is a lot safer in many respects than European or North American cities.

Unfortunately, tourists do not have to be robbed at gun-point to be left with the feeling that their tropical paradise is not all it was cracked up to be. Many destinations have a problem with what is usually referred to as 'visitor harassment.' This can range from the comparatively mild, such as the way in which any white person walking around the centre of many Caribbean cities will be assumed to be in immediate need of a taxi, to the rather more unpleasant, such as having one's efforts to sunbathe peacefully on the beach repeatedly interrupted by 'shoreline executives' with briefcases full of shell jewellery or bottles of home-made aloe vera sun-lotion – some of them may indeed be selling no more than shell jewellery or aloes, but others use this as a cover for offering drugs and sex (with graphic descriptions as part of the sales pitch). Most of the time a polite 'no thank you' will work, but sometimes the uninterested visitor is treated to a volley of insults. There are of course beach vendors who are neither unduly persistent nor offering anything illegal, and visitors sometimes report friendly conversations with them as a highlight of their stay.

There are always some visitors who are interested in buying what others would rather decline. Local papers regularly report incidents of tourists getting caught and fined for small quantities of illegal drugs, as well as more occasional cases of those apprehended while attempting to smuggle larger amounts into or out of the country – a long jail term is the usual consequence.

Most destinations have a fairly visible sex industry, which covers not only straightforward prostitution, but also the more ambivalent system of a visitor acquiring a temporary boyfriend or girlfriend for the duration of their stay from among those locals who make themselves available for the purpose. This can involve mutual attraction and respect, and is seldom a simple exchange of cash for sex. Nevertheless, the two parties often have different views of what the relationship means. The visitor might want what they see as just a bit of fun, while the local has a lingering hope that one day this sort of thing will lead to something more permanent involving a plane ticket and the right to emigrate, or at least the enjoyment of an extended holiday in the 'friend's' country at their expense. This, and the economic disparity between the two, mean that there is often a degree of manipulation and exploitation on both sides.

There are places in the Caribbean where teenage prostitutes hang around the bars and lobbies of five-star hotels, apparently with the permission or at least indifference of the management. In other places, signs saying things like 'No unregistered guests allowed in rooms' are intended to ensure that – if one is a hotel guest and the other is a local – two consenting adults do not get up to whatever they have a mind to, or at least not on the premises.

Both of these situations have their origin in the widespread belief that tourists are invariably richer than locals and that is therefore almost a moral duty on the part of the locals to milk them of their cash whenever possible. The secretary from Birmingham or the supermarket cashier from New York who has saved for a year or more for her two weeks of winter sunshine is probably not much – if at all – better off than many of her Caribbean counterparts, but the belief is a persistent one. It is certainly perpetuated by the minority of tourists who draw attention to themselves in an ostentatious manner. Algernon Aspinall, author of an early 20th-century guidebook which remained popular for many years, warned that 'Tourists will be well advised not to make themselves too conspicuous with puggarees and similar eccentricities as cabmen and boatmen naturally consider them to be fair game, and deal with them accordingly.' The modern equivalent is the fat gentleman I once saw sunbathing on a deck-chair on the beach in front of one of the most expensive hotels in Barbados, smoking a large

Children hustle a German tourist,
Santo Domingo, Dominican Republic

Philip Wolmuth

cigar and reading a book called *The Pursuit of Power*, but the principle remains the same.

Other problems are caused by the way in which the Caribbean is promoted. Some of this is done by foreign-owned hotel corporations, but it cannot all be blamed on outsiders; for decades a large part of the promotion of the region has been done by tourist boards which are predominantly local in composition. If a foreign advertising agency has been employed to create a campaign on the (entirely reasonable) grounds that it has a better knowledge of the target market, the tourist board, as the client, still has the responsibility for deciding whether or not to approve it.

Some early 20th-century postcards of Barbados showed 'The Haunted Wood' and 'The Cannibal Canal.' These sights were invented by Mr. Pomeroy of the Marine Hotel for the amusement of his guests, with his gardeners taking the parts of the 'ghost' and the 'cannibals.' More recent versions of this sort of travesty range from the 'pirate cruises' popular with visitors to several parts of the Caribbean, to the woolly caps knitted in red, green and gold with artificial locks sewn round the brim which are offered to tourists in Jamaica. The Japanese visitors I saw sporting these while dancing to the music of Bob Marley at a Jamaica Tourist Board function in Kingston perhaps thought they were paying tribute to Jamaican or specifically Rastafarian culture, but the fact that Jamaicans themselves refer

53

to these items as 'mock-de-dread hats' suggests some more negative connotations.

Tourist boards put out posters and other reminders to persuade visitors to 'keep beachwear for the beach' and not wear scanty clothing for shopping in city centres, as locals find this sort of behaviour disrespectful and disconcerting. Yet the same tourist boards encourage it by advertising campaigns which work very hard to suggest that Caribbean holiday destinations are happy, carefree places where nobody, nobody at all, actually has to do any work. Tourists behave accordingly, and it is hardly surprising that as a result they sometimes fail to show their best side to locals. While the tourist boards of a number of Caribbean countries do make efforts to promote their cultural attractions, this is sometimes done in a way which many Caribbean people find unduly simplistic or even a distorted parody. In any case, it has to struggle to compete with the continuing promotion of sea, sun and sand, with its subtext of sexual fantasy. One is left with the gloomy conclusion that, all too often, Caribbean people and their visitors get the version of each other's culture which is least likely to promote any real understanding.

4. Men in trade are making money there

The merchants of Bridge Town at that time, and for many years subsequently, conducted their business upon principles very different from those which now generally prevail; no man, in fact, being ranked as a merchant who was not his own general importer. It was also an invariable rule among them not to engage in, or connive at, any thing like retail traffic with inferior dealers, their sales being always made on an extensive scale, thus creating a sort of middle-man, who purchasing in larger quantity, retailed them in smaller lots to the petty hucksters. Credit was very limited at this time, and almost exclusively confined to the accommodation of the planter, who in those days never thought of importing his plantation stores, or of shipping his crop, these being considered the exclusive rights of the merchant; and thus a reciprocal interest, as should ever be the case, was established between the landed and commercial interests.

J. W. Orderson, *Creoleana: Or, Social and Domestic Scenes and Incidents in Barbados in Days of Yore*, 1842 (describing the late 18th century)

There are good shops in Kingston, and I believe that men in trade are making money there. I cannot tell on what principle prices range themselves as compared with those in England. Some things are considerably cheaper than with us, and some much, very much dearer. A pair of excellent duck trousers, if I may be excused for alluding to them, cost me eighteen shillings when made to order. Whereas, a pair of evening white gloves could not be had under four-and-sixpence. That, at least, was the price charged, though I am bound to own that the shop-boy considerately returned me sixpence, discount for ready money. [...] 'Four-and-sixpence for white gloves!' I said; 'is not that high?' – 'Not at all, sir; by no means. We consider it rather cheap. But in Kingston, sir, you must not think about little economies.'

Anthony Trollope, *The West Indies and the Spanish Main*, 1859

Patterns of trade

In 1768 a Caribbean writer gave a long list of the goods imported from Britain into his own colony:

> ... chiefly woolen, linen, Manchester velvets, silk, iron, brass, copper, leather, laces for linen, hats, wigs, shoes, stockings, china, glass, earthen wares, pictures, clocks, watches, jewels, plate, gold and silver lace, medicines, oats, pease, beans, cheese, bacon, starch, oatmeal, gunpowder, bricks, tiles, lead, paint, oil, coals, cordage, sugar pots, and drips, hoops, pewter, soap, candles, snuff, cut tobacco, pipes, cards, refined sugar, wine, beer, ale, cyder, perry, spice, fruit, tea, pickles, guns, swords, pistols, walking canes, horses, mules, grindstones, paving-stones, books, toys, stationary, cutlery, Birmingham, and haberdashery wares, coaches, chariots, chaises, all sorts of houshold goods, &c. besides the supplies from Ireland, and the very considerable importations of timber, fish, &c. from the northern colonies ...

He went on to finish his list by referring to 'the trade to Madeira' (the West Indian planter of the 18th century was traditionally fond to excess of Madeira wine) and to the importation of slaves. For exports, he listed only sugar, rum and molasses, though there were a few other minor products he could have mentioned.

The slave trade was suppressed in the 19th century, with the last, illegal, cargoes reaching Cuba in the 1860s, long after 'the man-degrading mart' had been officially abolished. A bottle of Madeira wine will occasionally still be found on the shelves of a Caribbean supermarket, but as an import from Britain, rather than a result of direct trade with Madeira. But much of the rest of the list is still imported into the region, with some variation: the coaches, chariots, and chaises have been replaced by motor-cars, and these are now more likely to come from Japan than from Britain or North America. Many of the other items are now imported, not from Britain, but from what used to be 'the northern colonies', that is, the USA and Canada. Guyana exports significant amounts of timber, but much of the lumber, plywood, and related products used in the Caribbean still comes from North America or, in more recent years, from Brazil. The briefest tour of a supermarket or department store in almost any Caribbean country will show how 'all sorts of houshold goods' are still imported to a very large extent.

While the manufacture of pottery for both use and ornament has been known in the region since Amerindian times – and has continued as an

Pottery vendor, Barbados, c.1930
Courtesy of John Gilmore

unbroken tradition in some territories – most of what is bought and used by local people is imported. Almost every Caribbean territory can boast both artists of distinction and local buyers of their work, but in many cases the artists would starve if they did not have other sources of income, such as teaching, and the interest of visitors in buying their paintings or sculptures, while local department stores continue to sell cheap mass-produced pictures and ornaments imported from outside the region. Leather-work is produced by individual craftsman, but while some of the larger countries like the Dominican Republic have managed to develop a shoe industry, most of the shoes you see being worn in the Eastern Caribbean will be either leather from Europe or South America, or cheap trainers from the Far East or expensive 'brand-name' trainers from North America. Anybody who has ever seen the amber jewellery produced in the Dominican Republic or the inside of a Chinese jeweller's shop in Paramaribo will know that some skilfully-made and extremely attractive jewellery is produced in the region, but local fine craft-work has to compete with imported mass-produced items such as die-stamped American eagle pendants and rolled-gold chains sold by the inch. The result is that some indigenous traditions, such as the intricate and varied gold filigree-work of Curaçao, are almost extinct.

Imports are not necessarily cheap. Statia's position in the 18th century as a free port, where European goods could be bought more cheaply than in Europe, proved to be both exceptional and temporary. A more usual situation was shown by the comments of G. J. Chester, an English clergyman who spent some time in the Caribbean in the mid-19th century, complaining of 'the exorbitant price charged for almost everything' in the shops of Bridgetown. The novelist Anthony Trollope was puzzled by the way in which some things seemed very cheap to him while others were very expensive, but the examples he chose were more revealing than he realised: his 'excellent duck trousers' were made in Jamaica, using skilled but cheap local labour, while the white gloves would have been imported ready-made and subjected to a considerable mark-up.

The patterns of trade and the dependence on metropolitan countries established in the period of sugar's greatest prosperity produced some important and long-lasting effects as far as both the individual consumer and the local economies in general in the Caribbean were concerned. The need to import almost all consumer goods led to a proliferation of middlemen – importer, wholesaler, distributor, shopkeeper, huckster – each of whom added on his (or, increasingly more likely as one got further down the scale, her) own profit. Credit may once have been 'almost exclusively confined to the accommodation of the planter,' but it spread right down the social scale after Emancipation, until it could be used for everything from the supplies for a 300-acre plantation to the half-cent in broken biscuits 'trusted' from the village shop by a mother anxious to keep her hungry children quiet but still several days away from receiving the miserably inadequate 'goods money' which was all her husband could afford to give her at the end of the week. Trollope got his sixpence discount for ready money, and Chester claimed it was said 'the storekeepers have so many bad accounts that they are obliged to charge high prices,' but in effect all consumers paid dearly for the widespread extension of credit. Development since the Second World War has meant better jobs and better wages for many more people, and with this a much greater reliance on cash payment. Nevertheless, many people still repair their houses with the help of a 'running account' at a hardware store, or buy furniture on credit from a department store. The traditional itinerant pedlar who became a feature of Caribbean life around the early years of the 20th century – stereotypically a Syrian with a cardboard suitcase, or, later, an East Indian with a van, selling dress material or ready-made garments for a small weekly payment which in the long run amounts to a very considerable mark-up – has survived into the present, and continues to exist alongside the quite recent introduction and growing popularity of North American or European-style credit cards issued by banks. What this all meant on a macro-economic level was the creation of an entrepreneurial culture based on buying and selling rather than on manufacture – it always used to be, and to a significant extent still is, much

Three of the Caribbean's major products over the centuries; rum, limes and sugar

John Gilmore

easier and safer to make money on an import-and-mark-up basis than by actually producing anything locally.

Manufacturing

Nevertheless, manufacturing of various kinds has existed in the Caribbean since the early days of the colonial period. Sugar has to be seen as an agro-industry, something which requires not only land and the people to till it, but a very considerable investment in buildings and sophisticated machinery to produce even the unrefined sugar which is exported for further processing elsewhere. (Refined sugar is still imported into the Caribbean.) Other traditional manufactures have ranged from artisan productions for local consumption, such as pottery and basketwork, to items based on local raw materials which have been either minor or major exports – pickles, preserves and relishes (including the many varieties of West Indian 'hot sauce') would fall into the former category, while rum and tobacco products (especially Cuban, Jamaican and Dominican Republic cigars) could be included in the latter. While sugar has long been in decline, rum has often been more successful. Puerto Rico's special relationship with the USA, massive advertising and the distilling of its product under licence in other countries have helped to make Bacardi rum the best-selling branded spirit in the world. Agreements with international producing or marketing companies have also been of help to some Caribbean distillers: currently all the alcohol

59

used in Malibu (a blended drink with large sales in many countries) is Barbadian rum.

However, Caribbean rum producers have faced difficulties arising from restrictive quotas and regulations in the European market, and rivalries between producers in the French islands of Martinique and Guadeloupe and those in the rest of the region. Other industries which involve at least partial processing of local raw materials are petroleum and natural gas in Trinidad, and bauxite in Guyana and Jamaica. Trinidad has had some success in expanding its oil industry to include the production of a variety of petrochemicals, and in using the availability of cheap energy from natural gas to develop an iron and steel industry using imported iron ore.

In more recent times, particularly since the 1950s and 1960s, a much wider range of industrial activity has developed. Many Caribbean countries now make commodities like bricks, tiles, and paint, soap and cosmetics, beer, and a range of manufactured food products like margarine, bacon, ham, confectionery and flour for local or regional consumption. Other non-traditional manufactures developed in recent decades include pharmaceuticals. Cuba has been particularly successful in this sector, a notable triumph being the development in 1985 of a meningitis vaccine which has not only greatly reduced what had been a serious health problem in Cuba itself, but which has also been exported on a large scale, with 40 million doses sold to 12 countries by 1998. The meningitis vaccine and other pharmaceutical products have become multi-million dollar earners of foreign exchange for Cuba.

However, where many products are concerned, the obvious drawback is the duplication of effort – just as most Caribbean territories produce similar agricultural products, so they produce similar manufactures. In the past, this difficulty has been overcome by protectionism, but the increased liberalisation of trade brought about by regional groupings such as Caricom has inevitably meant increased competition. It can be a nasty shock for a manufacturer of beer, soft drinks or ice-cream who has been accustomed to dominating their local market to be faced all of a sudden with significantly cheaper competing products imported from a neighbouring island, or even from outside the region. Unofficial arrangements can be equally devastating: apart from its curiosity value as, allegedly, the only beer in the world brewed from desalinated sea water, the Amstel beer produced in Curaçao is an excellent product with a very large share of the market not only in Curaçao but also in Aruba and Bonaire, but it has to compete with rival beers smuggled in from Venezuela and sold more cheaply.

Habits of consumption continue to be influenced by tradition. In an archipelago blessed with an abundance and variety of fish, an integral part of Caribbean cooking is salt fish imported from North America, even though decreasing stocks of Newfoundland cod mean that this is no longer the staple of the poor, but something of a luxury item. Local products of all kinds have to compete with what one might call the Johnny Walker syndrome – the local rum may be both excellent and cheap, but for many people it remains more prestigious to drink expensive imported Scotch. One of the comparative success stories of Caribbean industry has been clothing, which ranges from well-made but purely functional items, to one-off high-fashion pieces sold to wealthier locals and visitors. Caribbean clothing has to contend not only with changing regulations and quotas in countries such as the USA, on which it depends for much of its export market, but also on its domestic market's fondness for 'brand-name' clothes from extra-regional sources. I have seen a newly built hotel in a Caribbean island – owned by a Caribbean entrepreneur – which had used floor tiles imported from an extra-regional source, when almost identical tiles could have been obtained from a neighbouring island.

Pricing is affected not only by producers' and retailers' need and desire for profits, but also by a range of international agreements, government regulations and local circumstances which can make the relative costs of different items as bewildering to the consumer as Trollope found them. I have drunk canned Heineken (imported from the Netherlands) in the jungles of Suriname cheaper than I could get bottled Heineken (manufactured under licence in the neighbouring island of St. Lucia) in a rumshop in Bridgetown, Barbados. A Japanese car costs approximately twice as much in Barbados as the same model would if bought in the USA; the difference is largely due to the level of local tax on vehicles – not simply a revenue measure, as it is also intended to limit the number of vehicles on the crowded roads of a comparatively small island. In the English-speaking Caribbean countries, language is still too often seen as a barrier to opportunities which might be created in trade with Latin America and the Hispanic Caribbean. When you see that the Colombian coffee in your local supermarket has been imported by way of Britain or the USA instead of directly from Colombia, it is easy to understand the historical and other reasons for this sort of arrangement, but rather harder to believe that its persistence offers any advantage to the Caribbean consumer.

Caribbean countries are also home to many assembly industries, producing finished goods from imported components. These include consumer durables such as fridges, stoves and televisions for local and regional markets. An enormous variety of clothing is produced: while

Table 3: Top three exports of selected Caribbean countries and top three trading partners for each commodity (1997)

Country	Main Export	2nd	3rd	Main Export %	2nd %	3rd %
Barbados	Cane Sugar	Food Preparations	Electrical components	GBR 100	VEN 59.3 TTO 10.8 SUR 10.7	USA 88.5 GBR 9.7 HKG 0.8
Dominica	Soap and detergents	Soap cakes	Disinfectants	JAM 68.2 GUY 20.0 LCA 4.0	JAM 38.5 USA 18.3 TTO 13.4	JAM 71.9 BRB 8.9 TTO 7.3
Dominican Republic	Ferro Nickel	Cane sugar	Coffee	BLX 40.7 USA 22.0 KOR 20.0	USA 100	USA 53.4 CAN 12.2 ITA 11.2
Grenada	Nutmeg	Tunafish	Cocabeans	NLD 45.6 DEU 26.1 ARG 7.1	USA 100	NLD 40.8 GBR 26.1 BEL 18.1
Jamaica	Bauxite	Cane sugar	Clothing	CAN 27.5 NLD 21.5 NOR 12.3	GBR 83.1 USA 9.1 FRA 7.9	USA 99.1 CYM 0.3 BRB 0.2
St Lucia	Bananas	Cardboard boxes	Malt beer	GBR 100	TTO 70.8 BRB 9.2 SUR 6.7	BRB 26.2 DMA 17.0 ATG 15.2
St Kitts & Nevis	Cane sugar	Electrical switches	Electrical parts	GBR 60.1 USA 39.9	USA 100	USA 95.4 ITA 3.0 DEU 1.6
St Vincent	Bananas	Flour	Parboiled rice	GBR 96.1 TTO 3.9	LCA 42.6 ATG 18.4 KNA 14.5	JAM 23.8 LCA 23.8 ATG 16.9
Trinidad & Tobago	Petroleum oils (including crude)	Anhydrous ammonia	methyl alcohol (methanol)	USA 100	USA 83.5 BRA 3.8 CUB 3.0	USA 35.8 FRA 30.2 NLD 10.6

Source: Inter-American Development Bank

Country codes

ARG - Argentina
ATG - Antigua & Barbuda
BEL - Belgium
BLX - Belgium & Luxembourg
BRA - Brazil
BRB - Barbados

CAN - Canada
CUB - Cuba
CYM - Cayman Islands
DEU - Germany
DMA - Dominica
FRA - France
GBR - Great Britain

HKG - Hong Kong
ITA - Italy
JAM - Jamaica
KNA - St. Kitts & Nevis
KOR - Korea
LCA - St. Lucia
NLD - Netherlands

NOR - Norway
SUR - Suriname
TTO - Trinidad & Tobago
USA - United States of America
VEN - Venezuela

nearly all the textiles used are imported, the processing involved ranges from the sewing together of pieces imported ready cut, to local design and cutting, and elaborate hand-finishing such as smocking and embroidery work. Some of what is produced is sold within the Caribbean, but a large part of this industry depends on extra-regional exports. Like clothing, furniture industries are a development of traditionally widespread craft skills; most furniture produced in the Caribbean is bought by local consumers, though some firms have found niche markets outside the region for high quality reproductions of traditional designs. Other assembly industries primarily dependent on extra-regional exports include sporting goods and electronics.

Labour

All of this is based on the fact that labour costs in the Caribbean are lower, in some cases much lower, than in the countries to which these manufactures are exported. The extreme case is Haiti, where a 1997 study by the National Labor Committee (a US-based human rights group) of firms producing clothing under contract for the Walt Disney Company found that a Haitian worker received seven US cents for sewing a pair of Pocahontas pyjamas sold in the US for $11.97. Such a worker received an average wage of 28 US cents an hour, and would have had to work 156 years to earn as much as the CEO of Disney earned every hour in 1996.

A growing part of many Caribbean economies, in terms of both revenue and jobs provided, is formed by service industries – not just tourism, but also banking and insurance, data processing, and the provision of a range of specialised services from legal advice on how to make the most of a tax haven to the making of colour separations for the international printing industry. Some of the companies involved are not exactly labour-intensive – setting up a bank in some jurisdictions still requires little more than a brass plate and a post-office box – but others are major employers.

Some important players in the service industries are both long established and of local origin: institutions like the Barbados Mutual Life Assurance Society or Maduro and Curiel's Bank in the Netherlands Antilles are over 150 years old. However, this sector depends on a combination of factors which make the Caribbean attractive to outside investors. Not the least of these is a generally high level of political stability, but this would not be enough on its own.

Before the year 1867 it took about three weeks for news to travel from the Caribbean to Europe. The length of time depended to some extent on whereabout in the region you were. At best a message from Havana to London took about two weeks, while from Barbados to London it took more like three weeks and from Georgetown in British Guiana about one month. [...]

After telegraph communication was established between the Caribbean and Europe at the beginning of the 1870s, the time it took for a message to travel from one to the other was reduced to a couple of days, and by the beginning of the following decade one day was enough for a message to reach its destination. Communication between Canada or the United States and the Caribbean was then a matter of hours.

Jorma Ahvenainen, *The History of the Caribbean Telegraphs before the First World War*, 1996

A system of telephonic communication has been established in Barbados, and as the charge for hire of instrument and lines is very small (ten shillings a month), it is needless to say that great advantage is taken of it. Most of the better class of houses within a circuit of a couple of miles of the town are on the 'Telephone List,' and many far out in the country. Nowhere in the world has fuller advantage been taken of this invention than here, and the enterprise has succeeded to a remarkable degree, proving not only a great convenience to the public, but a profitable investment for the shareholders of the company who started it, who are receiving dividends of some twenty per cent. on their capital.

Rev. J. H. Sutton Moxley, *A West-Indian Sanatorium and a Guide to Barbados*, 1886

Communications, services and education

The Caribbean also enjoys excellent communications with the outside world; in relative terms, this has been true for centuries, but the last fifty years or so have seen even comparatively small islands like Aruba or St. Lucia acquire international airports and harbours capable of handling container traffic. Frequent air and sea services mean that, for both goods and passenger traffic, most parts of the region are easily accessible from North and South America, Europe, and the Pacific Rim. Effective telecommunications links with the rest of the world go back more than a century.

Life of Barbados insurance company headquarters *John Gilmore*

Some Caribbean territories introduced the telephone soon after its invention, and took to it with enthusiasm – the fact that in a number of islands the telephone subscriber has long enjoyed free local calls in exchange for a comparatively small monthly line rental has encouraged a widespread fondness for phone conversations of prodigious length. (As a result, Caribbean people who move to less fortunate metropolitan countries are sometimes appalled by their first phone bill.) Many can remember when an overseas phone call was a rare event, something which had to be specially booked through the operator for an occasion like Christmas or a birthday, but the introduction of improved technology means that much of the Caribbean now has access to the rest of the world through the most modern communications systems. International direct dialling, fax, the Internet and e-mail are now routine for many people, and in many Caribbean countries businesses can take advantage of the most up-to-date data transmission services.

Equally important is the way in which most Caribbean governments spend a large part of their budgets on education. An overseas investor can rely on a generally high level of literacy and on the availability of both skilled professionals in a wide range of fields and an educated work-force who can be fairly easily trained to perform new tasks. The use of English in Jamaica and the Eastern Caribbean is a plus, as is the fact that the whole of the region has no more than an hour or two's difference in time from the Eastern US and Canada. Icing on the cake is provided by the 'quality of life' details – the climate, the beaches, the golf courses, a normally adequate standard of public utilities and health care, the availability of domestic help – which make senior executives think a stint in the Caribbean not exactly a hardship posting.

But of course what makes a North American airline or insurance company move its data processing to a subsidiary in the Caribbean is the bottom-line justification. That such a company can have thousands of paper documents sent by courier to Jamaica or Barbados, have all relevant details keyed in overnight and get the resulting data sent back by satellite in digital form the next business day is simply a possibility. The reason the companies decide to act on the possibility is because the skilled, English-speaking labour necessary is obtainable in the Caribbean at considerably less than it would cost in the US or Canada. Further, Caribbean governments anxious to provide jobs for those who voted them into office extend generous concessions to investors ranging from ten year tax holidays for their companies to customs waivers so that their foreign managerial staff can import their cars duty free.

Frequent air and sea connections, and the high standard of telecommunications, have encouraged the development of free trade zones and entrepôt trade. This ranges from the import of luxury items such as perfumes and crystal for retail at duty free prices to tourists, to supplying the needs of wholesale buyers of almost any conceivable product. The larger free trade zones, such as those in Curaçao and at Colón in Panama, attract buyers from all over the Caribbean and Latin America. In addition, some assembly industries are located within free trade zones.

The same network of transportation connections, and the region's location, unfortunately make the Caribbean an important part of the international trade in illegal drugs. Some Caribbean countries produce significant quantities of marijuana (ganja) some of which is exported beyond the region, but this is a comparatively minor part of the problem. Since the 1980s, the Caribbean islands have become increasingly important as trans-shipment points for cocaine from South America. More recently, there has been a growth in the trans-shipment of heroin from South-East Asia through South America and the Caribbean. Drugs are smuggled into the Caribbean and then re-exported to destinations in North America and Europe by couriers using commercial passenger services, or by concealing packages of drugs in commercial cargo. An increasing amount is apparently sent through the region on fast boats designed to be virtually indetectable by radar, and which are owned and operated by the drug producers. The drugs trade is illegal in all Caribbean jurisdictions and causes growing problems from increasing local consumption of cocaine and its derivatives, particularly crack, and from corruption. Recognising the limited resources available to their Caribbean counterparts, North American and European governments have in recent years given increasing assistance to efforts to combat the trade.

Foreign investment

Manufacturing, assembly and service industries have made enormous contributions to the Caribbean. They have given jobs to thousands, and provided training and skill-development opportunities for Caribbean people. Foreign investment in such industries and the revenue generated from them directly and indirectly has enabled Caribbean countries to develop modern infrastructures and enjoy the benefits of improved standards of living in a way which would otherwise have been impossible.

Unfortunately, while there has been significant growth in local investment in all sectors, large parts of Caribbean economies are still under foreign control. It can be argued that some aspects of development actually increase the region's dependence on the outside world.

The growth of brewing in the Caribbean has meant that beer is no longer seen as an imported luxury, and that rum is no longer the only alcoholic drink available to many people. This may have health benefits, but rum is an entirely indigenous product (or was, until the decline of cane cultivation and sugar production obliged a number of rum-manufacturing countries to start importing molasses), whereas brewing requires imported grain and hops. Virtually every country in the English-speaking Caribbean has a flour mill which produces flour for baking and animal feeds from the by-products. Most of these mills were started as a result of Canadian investment, and some still have at least partly Canadian ownership; while the countries in which they are situated can buy locally produced flour and animal feeds instead of imported, they are still tied to the importation of wheat. Consumption of indigenous alternatives such as cassava has declined as the mills have encouraged changes in taste and increased dependence on imported raw material. The proliferation of service industries requires the constant importation of computers and other specialised electronic equipment which the Caribbean does not produce.

Relationships between foreign investors and Caribbean governments and peoples are nearly always one-sided – the Caribbean needs the investor more than the investor needs them. Tax and other concessions can persuade an investor that it will pay them to set up business in a particular territory, but investors can and do pull out when the concessions expire. Any hint of trade union militancy or demands for higher wages can set investors thinking that their products can be assembled more cheaply elsewhere, in a different Caribbean country, or perhaps in a Mexico which benefits from

NAFTA – or to thinking that while skilled, English-speaking labour is obtainable in the Caribbean at considerably less than it would cost in the US or Canada, it can be obtained for still less in other parts of the world, such as India.

Any suggestion of political instability is also disastrous, as was shown in Haiti in 1986, when many foreign companies left after the fall of the Duvalier regime, leaving thousands of Haitians out of work. All businesses in the Caribbean, whether locally or foreign owned, are vulnerable to circumstances over which Caribbean governments have little or no control: a rise in oil prices, a decline in demand for aluminium which reduces the demand for Jamaican and Guyanese bauxite, a change in US taxation policies which reduces the attractions of an off-shore account in the Caribbean, or eliminates the advantages of refining oil from extra-regional sources in the Caribbean for the US market.

In the late 1980s and early 1990s, the government of Guyana gave logging concessions to a number of companies, both Guyanese and foreign, but with a high proportion going to South-East Asian companies. Questions were raised about both the potential environmental impact and the fact that the concesssions were granted on on extremely generous terms, but the opening up of the country's forests was justified by the need for foreign investment and jobs. Certainly Guyana received some short-term benefits: the Barama Company Ltd., a joint Malaysian/South Korean venture which enjoys the largest concession, was employing nearly 1,000 people in the mid-1990s, a significant figure in a country with a total population of about 750,000. However, the downturn in the Asian economies in 1998 affected major markets for exports of Guyanese timber, and Barama and other companies were quick to lay off large numbers of workers.

Financial services

The need for foreign investment can lead countries to permit the establishment of individual enterprises or whole categories of businesses which can be seen as creating ethical dilemmas or practical problems. The obvious example is the way in which the development of the offshore financial industry has led to accusations that the Caribbean plays an important role in international money-laundering. A number of Caribbean countries have introduced more sophisticated regulations to combat this, and closed down many of the more dubious banks and offshore financial institutions, but there is always the problem that the governments of small countries simply do not have the resources to carry out elaborate checks on an international scale to verify the bona fides of every potential investor.

In Barbados, any suggestion that the government is about to permit casino gambling meets with considerable public protest, but in 1998 Barbados was embarrassed when James Blair Down, a Canadian entrepreneur, pleaded guilty in a US court to conspiring to violate federal anti-gambling laws.   Down had used a telemarketing business he had established in Barbados as a base for an operation selling lottery tickets which had, according to US investigators, swindled hundreds of elderly Americans out of sums totalling more than US$150 million.   This was not the end of the Caribbean's involvement, for Down had then laundered the proceeds through a large number of bank accounts not only in the US, Canada, Switzerland, and the Channel Islands, but also in the Cayman Islands, while the house in which he lived in Barbados had been bought by an offshore company in the British Virgin Islands, which Down was believed to own. The Barbados authorities have since moved to tighten up regulations governing international businesses established in the island.

In spite of the problems, the Caribbean will continue to need foreign investment.   It also needs to continue to develop its own expertise to ensure a better balance between local needs and a reasonable return for the foreign investor.   Complete self-sufficiency for any country in the modern world is an illusion.   The late President Forbes Burnham's attempts to force Guyanese to eat rice flour instead of wheat flour and to use local substitutes for other imported foodstuffs (or do without) were little more than covering a disastrous mismanagement of the economy in a veil of propaganda, and the response of many Guyanese was a combination of ridicule and smuggling. Caribbean countries are not unique in being affected by trends and events outside their borders, but their small size makes them particularly vulnerable.   For example, when in 1985 changes in the world market for oil led Exxon to close down the Lago refinery operated by a subsidiary in Aruba, this meant the end of what had been not only at one point the largest oil refinery in the world, but also the island's largest employer and largest source of income for more than fifty years.   This could have been a disaster, but the Aruban government decided to make a switch to tourism, as the alternative which offered the greatest potential for increasing both direct and indirect employment.   Modernisation of the island's infrastructure, the construction of new hotels, and some excellent marketing succeeded in doubling the number of visitors to the island in a few years – the economic and employment crisis caused by the Lago closure proved to be temporary, and Aruba soon came to be an importer of labour.   When every allowance is made for the fact that this depended on attracting massive foreign investment, as well as outright gifts, such as the European Union grant which paid for a new airport, it shows the enterprise and resilience of which Caribbean people are capable.

5. Après Bondie, c'est la Ter

Your grownd & plantations shewes whatt you are, they lye like ye ruines of some village lately burned, – heer a great timber tree half burned, in an other place a rafter singed all black. Ther stands a stubb of a tree above two yeards high, all ye earth covered black wth cenders nothinge is cleer. What digged or weeded for beautye? All are bushes, & long grasse, all thinges carryinge ye face of a desolate & disorderly shew to ye beholder.

Sir Henry Colt, describing the Barbadian landscape in 1631.

It is estimated that between the discovery of the tailings pond breach on the morning of 20 August and its final sealing on 24 August, some 128 million gallons of cyanide-laced gold mining waste poured into the Omai River from the largest gold mine in South America.

Omai Gold Mines Limited (OGML) officials admit that they hauled at least 300 dead fish out of the Omai River, which scientists have referred to as being 'dead,' with all aquatic life poisoned by the high concentration of cyanide which has escaped into it.

The millions of gallons of cyanide waste has also significantly changed the colour of the rest of the Essequibo River (into which the Omai flows) for some 90 miles downstream to Bartica.

But company officials insist that the cyanide contamination is not at dangerous levels and the river water is good for human consumption – a point which contradicts local Health Ministry warnings against consumption of water, fish, or shrimp from anywhere along that section of Guyana's largest and longest river.

Earl Bousquet, *Caribbean Week*, 2-15 September 1995.

Après Bondie, c'est la Ter ('After God, the Land')
Motto on the national coat of arms of the Commonwealth of Dominica

Fragile beauty

The beauty of the Caribbean is a cliché which goes back to Columbus, whose reaction to his first sight of Cuba was to say that 'it was such a great joy to see the plants and trees and to hear the birds singing that he could not leave them and return.' Five centuries later, the Caribbean is still capable of astonishing natural beauty, from the spectacular scenery of Jamaica's Blue Mountains to the more sedate attractions of watching birds scuttle across the pink, mauve and white tints of the salt-ponds of St. Kitts' south-east peninsula. Columbus wondered at the 'marvellous variety of large and small birds very different from our own,' and at the 'trees ... of many kinds, each with its own fruit.' Even today a cursory examination reveals that nature in the Caribbean is much more than an undifferentiated mass of lush greenery: the region's islands have a total land mass roughly that of the state of Oregon, but nearly as many different vertebrate species as the whole of the United States and Canada.

Some isolated places show a truly remarkable biodiversity: a 1998 research expedition discovered some 950 different terrestrial species of animals and plants on the two square miles of Navassa Island, 40 miles west of Haiti. Of these, some 800 were previously unrecorded on the island and it was estimated that as many as 250 species might prove to be endemic. More than 100 species of lichens were collected, though no lichens at all had been reported before. This is in spite of the fact that in the 19th century Navassa was extensively mined for its deposits of guano, which were exported to the United States for use as fertiliser. Off the southern coast of St. Lucia, the two tiny Maria Islands are home to a number of different species of bird and reptile, including the *zandoli tè* (*Cnemidophorus vanzoi*), a lizard found nowhere else in the world; the larger of the two, less than 25 acres in extent, is the only place where the *kouwès* snake (*Dromicus ornatus*) survives.

But the beauty of the Caribbean is extremely fragile, and both the terrestrial and marine environments of the islands and the surrounding continental countries have been extensively and brutally altered by human intervention since the time of Columbus.

The 'Destruction of the Indies'

Columbus did not, of course, arrive in an uninhabited wilderness. The size of the pre-contact Amerindian population continues to be a matter of debate among historians, but one figure, much repeated in the 16th century and based on an attempt by the Spanish at a systematic collection of tribute in 1496, was one million, one hundred thousand people (male and female, between the ages of 14 and 70) for the bare half or thereabouts of the island of Hispaniola then under Spanish control. Bartolomé de las Casas (1484-1576), who devoted much of his life to denouncing the human cost of the Spanish conquest, 'the Destruction of the Indies,' has often been accused of exaggerating for propaganda purposes, but his estimate of the Amerindian population of Hispaniola as more than three million may not be all that far from the truth. Today the same island (the present Haiti and the Dominican Republic) has a population of about fifteen million; in comparison, the Amerindian population, though much smaller, was still substantial.

The only metal the Amerindians knew how to work (and then only in the Greater Antilles) was gold, which served only for purposes of ornament, though a few objects of guanín, a gold alloy, appear to have been obtained by trade with mainland territories. Their only tools were made from wood, stone and shell. However, they were able to support themselves by combining hunting and fishing (including the catching of turtles) with an intensive agriculture based largely on cassava, a root crop which surpasses even the potato in the amount of nourishment which it can provide from a given area of land. By growing cassava in mounds together with a variety of other crops which restored nutrients to the soil and kept the mounds together, the Amerindians prevented both soil erosion and exhaustion. They attributed cassava to a divine gift; by luck or experiment they had discovered a system of living whereby they were able to exploit their environment without destroying it.

In the Greater Antilles, all this had been swept away within a few decades. The Amerindian population was devastated, not so much by deliberate massacre (though this did occur at times), as by the introduction of European diseases and by Spanish demands for forced labour, which prevented their maintaining their traditional methods of cultivation and so destroyed their ability to feed themselves. Whatever the numbers of the indigenous peoples might have been in 1492, all observers were agreed that, only a few decades later, they had dwindled to vanishing point. In 1514 the Spanish could count only 22,726 able-bodied Indians in Hispaniola, excluding children and the aged. By 1519, most of the surviving Indians in Hispaniola had died of smallpox.

Nor did the Spanish put much in place of what had been destroyed. The discovery and conquest of the much greater wealth of Mexico and Peru reduced the islands of the Caribbean to the status of an imperial back-water. They retained a usefulness as transit points, and as cattle ranches, supplying food and hides to the mainland, but in the late 16th century an official estimate put the total number of Spanish settlers in Hispaniola, Cuba, Puerto Rico and Jamaica at less than fifteen hundred. Much of the areas which had been cultivated by the Amerindians reverted to bush. The Spanish saw no economic potential in the smaller islands of the Eastern Caribbean, and there the Amerindian peoples, generally referred to as Caribs, survived largely unmolested for a while longer, protected by the reputation which they enjoyed among the Europeans as a more aggressive race than their exterminated cousins of the Greater Antilles.

This began to change in the 17th century with the arrival of other European powers. English and French settlement in St. Kitts in the 1620s was soon followed by the massacre of the local Caribs, inaugurating a process by which the island Caribs were reduced to a handful of survivors in Dominica, St. Vincent and Trinidad by the end of the 18th century.

Export crops and environmental damage

The new European settlers resumed a policy which had been virtually abandoned by the Spanish in the Greater Antilles, and began to clear large areas of the smaller islands for the cultivation of export crops. In 1631, Sir Henry Colt described Barbados in terms which remind the modern reader of the way in which vast sections of the Amazon forest are being cleared for 'development' today. Barbados was then still recently settled, and Colt claimed it was 'now ye trade of Cotton fills them all with hope.' The Sugar Revolution of the mid-17th century accelerated the process of change. By about 1680, virtually the whole of the original forest cover in Barbados had been destroyed – the only surviving portion, Turner's Hall Wood, is a mere 50 acres in extent – and while the small proprietor never entirely disappeared, most of the island was given over to sugar plantations.

The environmental damage was obvious even to contemporaries. By the later 17th century, there were complaints that Barbados was overpopulated, and that its soils were exhausted. A long-term solution was found in the cane-hole method of agriculture, the earliest surviving reference to which dates from 1708. Instead of the cane-cuttings being planted in trenches dug the entire length of the field, they were placed in shallow, square holes, with other crops (such as yams, peas, and maize) planted in the spaces between the holes. Even on quite steep slopes, the holes functioned like a form of terracing and broke the effects of rain-water run-off, while the other crops (which were timed so as not to interfere with the cane harvest) also helped to reduce erosion and increased the use of the available land. Manure was placed round the individual cane-plants in the holes, a practice which limited the extent to which it could be washed away. The cane-hole method demanded intensive labour, but it was effective in limiting the problems of erosion and soil-exhaustion which had come to plague the industry, and it survived into the 1960s. With cheap agricultural

74

Logging, British Guiana, c1920   *Courtesy of John Gilmore*

labour no longer abundant, cane is now planted in mechanically tilled furrows and the problem of erosion has returned, while the use of heavy mechanical equipment on comparatively thin soil also produces soil compaction.

From Barbados, intensive sugar cultivation, including the use of the cane-hole method, spread to other Caribbean territories. It became widespread in the British and French colonies, while the Dutch developed and expanded the sugar plantations which had been started in the Guianas in the mid-17th century by English settlers from Barbados. The profitability of sugar meant the clearing of virgin land on a wide scale, and nowhere was this more extensive than in Cuba, a late entrant into the world sugar economy. Until the later 18th century, Cuba was a comparatively minor producer, but the industry received considerable stimulus from first, the importation of large numbers of slaves during the British occupation of Havana (1762) and secondly, the fact that the Spanish crown's removal of restrictions on slave imports (1789) was almost immediately followed by the virtually complete destruction of the Haitian sugar industry, which had been the largest in the world until that country's war of independence (1791-1804). The Cubans were the first to recognise the importance of economies of scale, the first to apply steam power successfully to grinding canes (in 1797, though there were earlier attempts in Antigua and Jamaica) and the first to make extensive use of steam power both in the large new central sugar factories and for transporting the canes to them – the first modern central was built in Cuba in 1831. The result was not only Cuba's rapid advance to the position of the world's leading sugar producer, but extensive destruction of the island's forests, which were cut down and burnt as fuel for the expanding sugar industry.

The generally downward trend in the fortunes of cane sugar since the middle of the 19th century has led to further environmental change. It is no longer profitable to keep marginal land in sugar, and in some cases whole islands have abandoned cane cultivation. In Antigua, for example, the sugar industry was closed down in 1971, and much of what was once cane-growing land has simply been abandoned and now supports little more than some rough pasture and what Antiguans call cassy-bush (*Acacia farnesiana*), a thorny shrub of little use to either man or beast.

Alternative crops have not always been successful. In Montserrat and Nevis, cotton cultivation (now abandoned) led to major soil erosion in the 20th century. In the Windward Islands, the development of the banana industry and, later, fears of what would happen when preferential marketing arrangements were brought to an end and the desire to make as much money as possible while they lasted, led to soil erosion as banana cultivation was expanded up increasingly steep and unsuitable hill-sides. The development of bananas also meant heavy use of fertilisers and pesticides, often with little thought of environmental consequences.

Where sugar has survived, it depends on a much more intensive cultivation than used to be the case. Manuring has moved on from the animal dung on which the industry relied from the 17th century, or the bird guano which replaced it in the 19th, to the use of modern chemical fertilisers. Similarly, getting gangs of slaves to wash the cane plants leaf by leaf with sea-water in the attempt to get rid of the 'blast' caused by an insect pest (*Aphis saccharina*), has been replaced with more sophisticated pesticides. These things work. Unfortunately, they have often been over-generously applied, with the result than the next heavy shower of rain carries much of them downhill to the sea, where they help pollution from other sources to kill off coral reefs and damage the marine environment. Pesticides also damage bird and insect populations. Abandoning sugar is not necessarily any better from an environmental point of view. Cane roots keep the soil together and can help to prevent erosion. Taking marginal hillsides out of sugar cultivation often means that the land is not put into another crop, but allowed to become rough pasture, where heavy grazing by sheep and goats leads to extensive loss of soil. Turning flatter cane land into housing developments or golf courses – increasingly popular in some islands which are seeking to expand their tourism – puts other demands on the environment. Golf courses need intensive cultivation and use a great deal of water.

Environmental conflicts:
population growth and tourism

Most of the Caribbean has seen a steady growth in population at least since the early 19th century. As well as the human problems caused by over-crowding, urban expansion has placed other demands on the environment, by taking land out of agricultural production, by increasing the need for water supplies, and by increasing the problems of waste disposal. In 1998, a government minister in Jamaica noted that the country produced some 2,220 tonnes of domestic solid waste and 16,000 tonnes of commercial and industrial waste every day, but that only 60% was being collected, saying 'The remainder is disposed of by way of indiscriminate dumping in gullies, open lots and wetlands.'

In the countryside, population growth in some countries has led to an expansion of traditional peasant economies beyond what the land can sustain. Forests are cut down to provide both fuel and land for cultivation, while the grazing of increased numbers of livestock has exacerbated the problems of erosion. The outstanding example is Haiti, which has lost most of its forests in the course of the 20th century, but other Caribbean territories face similar problems: in 1998 Jamaica was reported to have the highest rate of deforestation in the world, at 5.3% a year.

Many of Haiti's environmental problems can be attributed to the country's poverty, but prosperity brings its own hazards. The Scotland District of Barbados is a geologically unstable area, notoriously prone to land slippages. For many years, the area's inhabitants survived mainly on subsistence agriculture and work on neighbouring plantations, and lived in small wooden houses which had only limited impact on the environment. From the 1960s they began, like other Barbadians, to share in the benefits of a developing economy; they found better employment in other parts of the island, but many preferred to continue living in the district in which they had been brought up. They improved their existing homes or built new ones, adding modern conveniences. The unstable soils on steep hillsides which had been able to tolerate the traditional wooden houses were much less suited to bigger, cement-block homes, and land slippage became an increasing problem. As one local conservationist put it, 'Every time a toilet flushes, they're flushing themselves down the hill.' Matters were made worse by the use of tractor-ploughing instead of cane-holing in local agriculture, and by the end of the 1990s, the government was forced to plan the resettlement of the entire village of White Hill.

The need to provide a better standard of living for their peoples has led Caribbean countries to allow or encourage the growth of manufacturing

Maroon village, Suriname   *John Gilmore*

and extractive industries, and of tourism. Few industries are clean, and some are particularly damaging to the environment. Processing Jamaican bauxite to produce alumina (aluminium oxide) involves the use of caustic soda, some of which remains in the 'red mud' left behind after the alumina has been extracted, and this can pollute water supplies. For every tonne of alumina produced, there is five tonnes of red mud to dispose of. Small scale production of gold in Guyana leads to the pollution of rivers with the mercury used in the process, and larger gold-mining operations have their own dangers, as was shown by the spillage of millions of gallons of cyanide-contaminated waste into the Essequibo River in August 1995. For much of the 20th century, a large part of Guyana's forests was protected by its inaccessibility, but developments in transportation and technology, and the granting of very large logging concessions by the government from the late 1980s, have raised serious questions as to how far the exploitation of forest resources can be sustained, with environmentalists arguing that logging companies' claims about times needed for regrowth of cut areas are unrealistically optimistic.

In both Guyana and Suriname, the greatly increased importance of mining and timber industries has brought about a conflict of interest between the coastal population and the traditional dwellers in the forest – the Amerindian peoples and also, in Suriname, the Maroons (descendants of slaves who escaped from the sugar plantations in the 17th and 18th centuries and who have successfully preserved a distinctive culture). The forest dwellers point out that the destruction of their environment by excessive logging and the pollution of the rivers in which they fish amounts to the destruction of their way of life. The much larger coastal populations either give little thought to the interior at all, or think only of the potential gains to be made from its exploitation. The forest dwellers are too often seen as a minority who cannot be allowed to stand in the way of 'progress' and reminders that the Amerindians were the original inhabitants of the country who have been largely dispossessed by the later arrivals tend to be dismissed as irrelevant.

Tourism adds its own problems by putting increased pressure on water resources and waste disposal systems. There are still places where hotels pump untreated sewage straight into the sea. On a more positive note, after considerable negative publicity in recent years, the cruise-ship industry seems to have become more environmentally conscious, with the introduction of on-board recycling and other measures to reduce waste. Demand for both domestic and hotel-sector construction has led to environmentally damaging mining of beach sand in some islands. Eco-tourism and heritage tourism have been increasingly advocated in recent years as 'greener' alternatives, but it is probably difficult to prevent these from overstepping the point at which the number of visitors is enough to damage the very things they have come to see. If you take too many visitors up rivers and around mangrove swamps in motorised boats to admire the wildlife, sooner or later the wash from the motors will erode the banks and churn up the water to the point where delicate ecosystems are damaged and the wildlife will disappear.

Not everything can be blamed on the tourists themselves. I have seen a bulldozer being used to remove gravel from the banks of the Rio Grande in Jamaica, in full view of tourists and visiting travel writers to whom the river was being promoted as part of the island's unspoilt charms. The built environment, the heritage of historic and architecturally interesting buildings, is increasingly being marketed as a significant aspect of the region's attractions. The Caribbean still possesses a great deal that is truly outstanding in this respect, but much has been destroyed as a result of local people's indifference or the short-sighted pursuit of immediate gain. The fact that the scarlet ibis, one of Trinidad and Tobago's national symbols, no longer breeds in the Caroni Swamp is probably to be attributed as much to environmental pollution from other causes as to an excess of visitors coming to look at their spectacular dawn and dusk flights.

Blow, winds, and crack your cheeks! rage, blow!
You cataracts and hurricanoes, spout
Till you have drench'd our steeples, drown'd the cocks!

William Shakespeare, *The Tragedy of King Lear* (c. 1605), Act III, Scene ii.

The fury of the tempest encreased with the approach of night; and a scene of terror and distress awaited the ruined and dismayed inhabitants in the dread hour of darkness, of which no powers of language can convey an adequate idea [...] Early in the evening the cattle had, in some places, broken from their folds, and with dismal bellowings sought refuge among the habitations of men. But these, alas! afforded a doubtful shelter to their possessors; who, to save themselves from being crushed to death, or, which was more horrible, from a premature interment under their falling mansions, fled for safety to the open fields. Each, ignorant of the other's fate, thought his neighbour more fortunate than himself; and flying from certain death beneath his own crumbling walls, sought an asylum, which, in that universal scene of desolation, was nowhere to be found. The author of this narrative was himself, with his wife grievously contused by the fall of his house, and an infant daughter, only six months old, among the midnight wanderers, who traversed the dreary waste in search of an uncertain place of shelter and repose.

John Poyer, *The History of Barbados* (1808), describing the hurricane of 1780.

Natural disasters

No account of the Caribbean environment could ignore the region's propensity to natural disasters. It is not for nothing that the English language acquired the word 'hurricane' from a Carib source. The geographical position and geological origins of the Caribbean islands mean that many of them are at risk from hurricanes, earthquakes and volcanic eruptions, and the region has seen some spectacular disasters, such as the earthquake and tidal waves which in 1692 destroyed the town of Port Royal in Jamaica with the loss of 2,000 lives, or the 1902 eruption of Mount Pelée in Martinique, which in a few minutes obliterated St.-Pierre, the 'Paris of the Antilles,' killing 30,000 people. In the same year, an eruption of the Soufrière volcano in St. Vincent caused 2,000 deaths.

Such events often affect more than one territory: hurricanes regularly sweep through several islands leaving a trail of destruction before causing

Town of St Pierre, Martinique, c1901, before its destruction by the smoking volcano in the background

Courtesy of John Gilmore

further devastation on the mainland of Central or North America or spending the last of their forces harmlessly in the middle of the North Atlantic. An earthquake in 1843 left Guadeloupe by far the worst affected, with some 5,000 people killed in that island, but it also caused damage and loss of life in Antigua, Montserrat and Dominica. On the other hand, there can be useful side-effects – the soils of Barbados, which is a coral rather than a volcanic island, have benefited significantly over the centuries from the deposition of large quantities of volcanic ash from eruptions in neighbouring islands.

While damage to property from such events remains considerable, loss of life is generally much less than it used to be. The 1780 hurricane was said to have killed three or four thousand people in Barbados, while that of 1831 left some 1,500 dead in the same island. Deaths on this scale were due to the fact that, before the development of modern meteorology, there was often little more than a few hours' warning of the approach of a hurricane. By contrast, when Hurricane Janet hit Barbados in 1955, the population had been able to take precautions, and, although there was severe damage, and some 20,000 people were left homeless, there were only 35 deaths. A series of volcanic-related earthquake sequences in the first half of the 20th century led to the setting up in 1952 of what became the Seismic Research Unit in Trinidad (since 1961 part of the University of the West Indies). In 1971 and again in 1972, the Seismic Research Unit was able to warn the government of St. Vincent of impending volcanic

81

eruption – the eruptions occurred as predicted, but no lives were lost. There are other seismological observatories in Jamaica, and in the French and Hispanic Caribbean.

Nevertheless, in 1998 the Caribbean News Agency reported a survey by the International Federation of the Red Cross as estimating that 'Just under three-quarters of a million people in the Caribbean are affected by disasters annually.' While early warning enables people to take appropriate action, unfortunately the reverse is also true, and some natural disasters have been made worse by human error. In 1902 Mount Pelée showed clear signs of activity for some time before it erupted, but government authorities in Martinique chose to ignore the evidence of danger – an election was coming up and they wanted voters to stay in the town. When Hurricane Georges swept through the northern Caribbean in September 1998, causing death and destruction in half a dozen countries, officials in the Dominican Republic ignored advice from meteorologists and refused to issue warnings, with the result that most of the population was caught completely unprepared and the death toll (put by official figures at more than 200, though other sources claimed it was much higher) was far above that for other countries affected. One newspaper in the Dominican Republic claimed it had sought to publish details of hurricane shelters so that its readers could take refuge in them before Georges struck, only to be told by officials that the list of shelters was confidential, and that when the hurricane arrived would be time enough to release it.

The region is not the only part of the world to suffer from natural disasters, but the small size of most Caribbean countries makes them particularly vulnerable. While electricity and water supplies can normally be restored quite quickly after a hurricane, it takes longer to repair damaged housing stock. Some 85% of the housing stock in St. Kitts was damaged by Hurricane Georges, and the country's prime minister put total damage at US$445 million. One consequence is that companies and individuals in the Caribbean have to pay high rates for buildings insurance. Reports of disasters are bad publicity for the tourist industry, especially as many potential tourists cannot tell one end of the Caribbean from another, and the belief that a hurricane in one island means the entire region is affected leads to unnecessary cancellations. On the other hand, the fact that so many people outside the region never think about the Caribbean until it is time to start looking at their holiday brochures does mean that tourism normally recovers fairly rapidly. Whole industries can be devastated – in September 1995, the entire banana industry in Dominica was destroyed when the island was hit by two successive hurricanes in a week, while after

Main boulevard of Plymouth,   *Rob Huibers/Panos Pictures*
former capital of Montserrat, 1997

Hurricane Georges in 1998, it was reported that 90% of the citrus industry in the Dominican Republic had been destroyed.

The prime example of how a small country can be affected by events completely beyond human control is Montserrat. Although this is a volcanic island, there had been no evidence of activity from the Soufrière Hills Volcano in historic times. However, a series of seismic events beginning in 1992 was followed by eruptions of steam and ash from the volcano in 1995. Intensification of volcanic activity and associated earthquakes and landslides led to some twenty deaths, the destruction of the airport and main sea-port, and the abandonment of two-thirds of the island, including the capital, Plymouth. What had been a comparatively prosperous economy based on tourism, agriculture and off-shore finance was ruined, and the majority of the population (11,200 before the eruptions began) was forced to leave, having seen their homes and livelihoods destroyed. The remaining 3,000 inhabitants were crammed into a small area in the north of the island. Considerable aid has come from overseas sources, particularly Britain (the island is still what is now called a British Overseas Territory, rather than a colony), and most Montserratians have a very strong attachment to their homeland.

There have been suggestions that eventually the volcano will prove to be a wonderful tourist attraction, and that the hundreds of thousands of tons of volcanic ash which have been dumped over the island might become a valuable resource, as the ash can be used to make building slabs and blocks. However, a scientific report issued at the end of 1997 pointed out that while there was little likelihood of real danger to the northern zone, and a truly catastrophic explosion which would destroy the entire island was extremely unlikely, it was probable that the volcano would continue to show much the same level of activity for 'a few more years.' While this is so, the future of Montserrat remains uncertain.

Lizards can be easily harmed by our unthinking actions. For example, littering poses a threat to lizards, who can enter discarded bottles, become trapped and die of heat exhaustion. One bottle found by Dr. Corke contained three dead lizards. Three such bottles could wipe out 1% of the total world population of *zandoli tè*. This is an important reason why visitors should be careful to avoid leaving bottles or other litter on the islands.

Maria Islands Nature Reserve: Interpretive Guide (1985).

Local extinctions

What makes the Caribbean attractive to so many people depends on climatic and geographical factors which produce a series of delicately balanced eco-systems which are all comparatively small and extremely vulnerable. At the same time, unfortunately, their very attractiveness increases their vulnerability. The apparent abundance of natural resources has again and again – as in other parts of the world – led to their exploitation to the point of extinction.

The mastic tree (*Sideroxylon foetidissimum*) was once a valuable timber species in Barbados, but only a single tree is now known in the island. The Caribbean monk seal (*Monachus tropicalis*) was a common marine mammal in the time of Columbus, but it was extensively hunted for food, and because it was believed to damage fish stocks; already rare by the 18th century, it is believed to have been extinct since about 1960. Turtle meat and turtle eggs were important items in the diet of the Amerindians, and Caribbean turtle became famous in Europe, with live turtles being shipped across the Atlantic to be turned into turtle soup for civic banquets and other grand occasions. All Caribbean turtle species are now endangered. Other plant and animal species have disappeared as a result of over-exploitation or of man-made changes in their environment. The list is a long one – one scientific authority has estimated that of all the vertebrate extinctions in the world which have occurred in historic times, 40% have taken place in the Caribbean.

In western Jamaica, the town of Negril is internationally famous for its beach – seven miles of white sand which attract many thousands of tourists every year, and which brought massive development in the 1980s, as large areas of wetlands were filled in so that hotels could be built. The sheer weight of the new structures has pushed the beach out to sea, so that large quantities of sand have been washed away. Marine pollution and damage caused by divers and the anchoring of tourist boats have left the offshore reef dying. Further damage caused by bad weather, such as Hurricane Gilbert (1988), has not helped, but essentially the town's tourist industry is rapidly destroying the attractions which created it in the first place. A 1998 study showed that in only three years 33 feet of the Negril beach had been washed away as a result of erosion.

All over the Caribbean, there is a greater awareness of conservation issues. Unfortunately, in many cases, those who express concern about the preservation of the natural or the built environment are still over-ruled by those for whom 'development' is still seen as an unmitigated good. In 1993, when an Italian company began clearing ecologically valuable mangrove wetlands at Coconut Hall in Antigua for a tourism development project, there was considerable local protest. Official response included a statement in parliament by the country's Agriculture, Lands and Fisheries minister, that 'We're going to rest the hammer on these environmentalists, show them who has the power,' while the prime minister, Vere Bird, Sr., commented in a radio interview that 'When people lie down in front of bulldozers, sometimes bulldozers run them over.' Things are seldom put so bluntly, but those responsible for decisions affecting the environment often seem to feel that conservationists are a nuisance which can be safely ignored. An outstanding example occurred in St. Lucia in the early 1990s, when it was proposed to build a luxury resort between the Pitons – two dramatic volcanic cones revered as a national symbol. This aroused widespread protest and was condemned in strong terms by the country's most famous voice, the poet Derek Walcott, but the project went ahead nevertheless.

6. Cane is bitter

Why did all-creating Nature
    Make the plant for which we toil?
Sighs must fan it, tears must water,
    Sweat of ours must dress the soil.
Think, ye masters, iron-hearted,
Lolling at your jovial boards;
Think how many backs have smarted
For the sweets your cane affords.

William Cowper, 'The Negro's Complaint' (1788).

Sugar and suffering

In a famous short story from the 1950s called 'Cane is Bitter,' Samuel Selvon drew a grim picture of the narrow, inward-looking lives of an East Indian family in rural Trinidad whose poverty forces them to carry on cutting and piling canes, scarcely able to imagine any escape. The parents have sent the eldest son, Romesh, to school in Port of Spain, but while his mother says 'One day he might come lawyer or doctor, and all of we would live in a big house in the town, and have servants to look after we,' his father dismisses this as 'foolish talk.' They are afraid of how the city has changed him – 'Suppose he want to take creole wife?' – and they 'want help on the estate.' When Romesh comes home for the school holiday, he discovers they have arranged for him to marry a village girl who will bring him a good dowry. His mother tells him: 'Is the way of our people, is we custom from long time. And you is Indian? The city fool your brains, but you will get back accustom after you married and have children.'

Romesh rebels against what he calls 'such a low form of existence,' and refuses to marry the girl, saying that he will stay to help cut canes until the crop is over, but that he will leave afterwards. The reader is left thinking that perhaps he will – though wondering how Romesh will pay for the further education he so desperately wants if his parents can't or won't help him any more – but it is clear that he will only get away from the 'path pointed out' for him at the cost of rejecting his family and the people among whom he has grown up.

Europe's demand for the sweetness of sugar dominated the economies of much of the Caribbean for three centuries. It also created a system of exploitation and racial division of labour which has left an enduring and bitter legacy.

Much of this is ultimately due to the nature of cane cultivation itself. A field demands a great deal of preparation before it is ready for planting. When the cane is fully grown, it has to be cut and taken to the mill and ground so that the juice can be extracted from the canes and processed so as to get sugar out of it.

The growing and reaping are agricultural processes, while getting sugar out of the canes is an industrial process. There is no necessary or inevitable reason why the agricultural and industrial aspects should be undertaken by the same person or entity. Mediaeval England, for example, produced vast quantities of wool, but the English sheep farmer was not a manufacturer of cloth – English wool was mostly exported to the continent as a raw material. Similarly, in 17th-century Brazil, the capitalist who owned the mill, the *senhor do ingenio,* grew little or no cane himself, but was supplied with his canes by *lavradores*, who were small-holders or tenant-farmers.

From the late 19th century, parts of the English-speaking Caribbean have seen the growth in importance of cane-farmers, who are not planters in the traditional sense, but owners or renters of comparatively small pieces of land who grow canes and sell them to the factory. The increasing importance of central factories meant that even planters who used to grind their own cane found it more economic to send their cane to a larger and more modern factory, which might, indeed, have been established by such a planter and some of his colleagues joining together to subscribe some or all of the needed capital.

However, for the greater part of sugar's history in the Caribbean, the agricultural and industrial aspects were normally under the same ownership. The planter owned the land on which the canes were grown, and he also owned the mill in which they were ground and the boiling house and curing house in which the sugar was produced. The fundamental reason lay in the fact that, while it is possible to produce sugar with some fairly basic equipment, in order to do so on any scale or to produce good quality sugar with reasonable consistency has always demanded technology which has been quite sophisticated by the standards of its own day. This was expensive: while it might have been possible to get started as a tobacco farmer in Barbados in the early years for only £2 (see Chapter 2), in 1663 the Derbyshire ironmaster George Sitwell noted that a set of iron rollers for grinding canes could cost £24. As early as 1647 in Barbados, Colonel Modiford paid £7,000 for a half-share in a large sugar plantation which was already established. There was no point in making such a large investment unless you could make it pay, and the most effective way of ensuring that enough canes were brought to your expensive mill to produce enough sugar to give a good return on your investment was to grow them yourself.

The reasons for this are to do with the nature of the cane plant. This is, or rather was, *Saccharum officinarum*, a plant whose geographical origins are probably to be found in the islands of the Pacific, but which was gradually moved westward by human agency to the Asiatic mainland, to the Mediterranean, the islands of the Atlantic like the Canaries, Madeira and São Tomé, and finally – with Columbus – to the Caribbean and the Americas. Nowadays, cultivated canes are complex interspecific hybrids and thousands of varieties have been bred and tried for commercial use, but until the later 18th century there was only one known variety, referred to by later writers as the Creole cane. This had two awkward characteristics. In the first place, it was never grown from seed, but instead was raised from cuttings. Secondly, it took more than a year to reach maturity.

Also important were the factors which fixed the length and time of the grinding season in the Caribbean:

– a 17th- or 18th-century mill and boiling house could only process so much cane in a day
– cane has to be ground as soon as possible after cutting or the juice will lose much of its sugar content
– while canes need adequate rainfall for growth, they are best cut in the dry season – not out of any concern for the workers but because otherwise the juice will tend to be watery and demand more fuel for boiling.
– finally, the planter would want to have his canes taken off and all his sugar made and ready for shipping before the onset of the hurricane season increased both risks and insurance costs. This more or less coincided with the beginning of rainy weather.

This meant that in general crop-time would begin not long after the Christmas holiday and end in July or August, though more modern methods make a shorter time possible. In Guyana, economies of scale and fertile soils allow two grinding seasons in the year, but this was a 19th-century development and remains exceptional.

The most important aspect of the agricultural side of the process was that it was extremely labour intensive. Cane-holing was done by hand, by men and women digging out the holes with hoes. Forks might have been

Tourists relax by a swimming pool next to a long-disused
sugar factory, Bequia, St Vincent and the Grenadines

John Gilmore

more efficient, and indeed came into general use for the purpose at a later period, but the hoe was the normal implement during slavery and for long afterwards. There were experiments with preparing the land by ploughing furrows from the 18th century onwards, and steam-ploughs were tried at various times from about the mid- 19th century, but it was a very long time before the plough completely displaced the hoe – the cane-hole method was still being practised in parts of Barbados until the 1960s. Digging a hole in the ground is hard work, and digging a hole with a hoe is considerably harder than using a fork or a spade. Why then use hoes instead of forks? Why dig holes instead of plough furrows? And, for that matter, why was it that the usual method of fertilising the fields was to have the manure carried out to them by gangs of workers with baskets on their heads?

As mentioned above (Chapter 5), the cane-hole system had certain ecological advantages. However, one of the main reasons for the long survival of the cane-hole and the dung basket is probably to be sought at the other end of the cycle. Canes have to be cut. Until comparatively recent times, this meant that they had to be cut by hand. Cane cutting machinery now exists, and in Barbados, for example, has been in regular use for some twenty years. Barbados, indeed, has been a pioneer in the development of such machinery. But it is only suitable for use on comparatively flat terrain. Even now, throughout the Caribbean, much cane is still cut by hand.

This involves using a cane-bill or machete, which is quite heavy in the hand. The cutter must bend down to cut the cane as close to the ground as possible, so as not waste anything. Then he or she stands up, cuts the top off the cane, strips the trash or dried leaves off the stalk, drops it, moves on to the next cane and repeats the process. It is someone else's job to bundle up the cut canes and take them to a cart or lorry for transport to the mill or factory. The normal working day during crop, as the cane-harvest is known, was and is from sunrise to sunset. 18th-century planters, or at least some of them, used to recommend that slaves be allowed an hour or two off for food and rest in the heat of the day; the modern cane-cutter is paid by the weight of canes cut rather than by the day, and does not take so long for lunch. Cutting cane for a living means ten or eleven hours backbreaking labour under a hot sun, six days a week, for perhaps six months of the year. In addition, the edges of the cane-trash are sharp enough to scratch the skin, and cane-fields tend to be home to cow-itch plants, stinging ants, centipedes and other hazards.

In 1996, a lady called Myra Brathwaite won Barbados' Queen of the Crop title for cutting more cane than any other female worker – 348 metric tonnes in the course of the crop season. The *Nation* newspaper quoted her as saying 'I enjoy cutting cane, and for the last 33 years it has given me a house and helped me to raise my six children [...] but cutting cane can also be a drag. It can take everything out of you.' Myra Brathwaite was 53 years old at the time. Her male counterpart, King of the Crop Tyrone Nicholls, cut 422 tonnes the same season.

This is the kind of work which the owners of sugar plantations have always had to get people to do for them, and the problem is the same for a modern government agricultural corporation as it was for the planter of two centuries ago. While prime ministers and priests have gone into the field in an attempt to demonstrate the dignity of agricultural labour, and workers like Myra Brathwaite and Tyrone Nicholls get their all-too-brief moment of glory once a year, most people remain unconvinced. Ever since the Sugar Revolution of the 17th century, cutting cane has been the kind of job which few people are prepared to do if they have any alternative, or at least prepared to do for the kind of wages normally on offer in their own territory. A large part of the history of sugar in the 20th-century Caribbean has been the history of migrant labour. Workers from the Anglophone Caribbean went to Cuba in the 1920s, Haitians went – and still go – to the Dominican Republic, 'small islanders' and Guyanese go to Barbados, while Bajans who don't want to cut cane in their own country will go and do so in Florida to get paid in US dollars.

Cutting cane by hand, Cuba   *Rolando Pujol, South American Pictures*

Canes not only have to be cut, they have to be cut when they're ready. This is the basic reason for the centuries-long attraction of unfree labour to the planter. At the beginning of the Sugar Revolution, this labour was provided mainly by white indentured servants imported from Europe. But if the white servant lived long enough to serve out his term of indentureship, he could find something else to do – the massive white emigration from Barbados in the mid- to late 17th -century was the ex-servants' verdict on the attractions of cane-cutting.

Slavery and sugar

It was the Africans' misfortune to be a cheap and readily available source of labour at exactly this point. After Emancipation, the pattern repeated itself. Only in exceptional circumstances, such as in Barbados (long one of the most densely populated parts of the globe), or, to a lesser extent, Antigua, was it possible to persuade a high proportion of the ex-slaves to continue as plantation labourers at the kind of wages the planters wished to offer, and even then, the ex-slaves migrated in their thousands to seek a better deal elsewhere.

White racists in the Caribbean and in Britain, such as Thomas Carlyle in his notorious 'Occasional Discourse on the Nigger Question' (1849), denounced black Jamaicans and Guyanese as lazy because they preferred to establish 'free villages' and support themselves as subsistence farmers rather than cut cane for a shilling a day or thereabouts. Indentured labour was brought in once more, from India this time, to provide the planter with workers he could control, and to offer a means of driving down the black workers' wages. Indian indentureship lasted until 1917 in Trinidad and British Guiana.

Asian indentured labour, whether from China or Indonesia, was also used as a substitute or replacement for the labour of black slaves in territories like Cuba and Suriname. From the first half of the 17th century to the first half of the 20th, a very large part of the sugar production of the Caribbean depended on some form of unfree labour. The same use of unfree labour can be seen at different historical periods in other parts of the world where sugar has been produced on a large scale for export: African slaves followed by Indian indentured workers in Mauritius (in a pattern similar to that of the Caribbean), Indian indentured workers in Fiji, British convicts and kidnapped Pacific islanders in Australia, the so-called 'culture system' in the Netherlands East Indies.

Once the planter had acquired control of enough unfree labour to ensure that his canes were cut when he wanted them cut, he had to face the problem that he did not need so much labour out of crop. Before Emancipation, one solution to this was to own fewer slaves than were needed, and to hire extra labour in croptime from someone who owned what was called a 'jobbing gang,' a group of slaves who had been bought as an investment for the express purpose of hiring them out to the plantations. Slaves in jobbing gangs had a notoriously hard time of it, as it was in the interest of the hirer to get as much work out of them as possible without any concern for their long-term welfare. After Emancipation, planters in a densely populated island like Barbados simply didn't pay people when there was no work for them to do, confident that their labour would still be available in crop.

But it was usually considered preferable to supply, as far as possible, all of a plantation's needs from its own resources. If the planter owned enough slaves to cut his canes, he had to keep them occupied the rest of the year, as if they had too much time to themselves, they might start to plot rebellion. This – as much as any simple, obstinate attachment to tradition – probably accounts for the persistence of seemingly illogical and wasteful methods of work, in spite of the fact that even in the mid-18th century a planter like Colonel Samuel Martin of Antigua recognised that the plough might be more efficient than the hoe, and the hand-cart than the dung-basket. Traditional methods make work, in freedom as well as slavery. One of the concerns of the trade union movement in the 20th-century Caribbean was that agricultural labourers should not be out of work for several months of the year. In Barbados, for example, plantation workers have now for many years been guaranteed by law a minimum of three days' work a week out of

Sugar mill, Barbados, c.1910   *Courtesy of John Gilmore*

crop-time – one consequence of this is that the hoe and the dung-basket can still be seen in use.

Once the canes are cut, they have to be ground, and the juice which is obtained has to be boiled to extract the sugar. A modern sugar factory requires not only sophisticated machinery and equipment, but also staff with considerable chemical and technological expertise. Even in the 17th century, however, the grinding and boiling process, unlike the planting and cutting of the canes, demanded skilled labour. How much lime to add to the boiling juice, exactly when to remove the syrup from the fire, were matters which demanded nicety of judgement and considerable experience. Getting these details right or wrong affected both the quantity and the quality of the sugar made. The head boiler was one of the most important men on any estate, and from an early date this task was universally entrusted to slaves. The grinding, boiling and production of sugar also needed other skilled workers – carpenters, mill-wrights and coopers.

The racial hierarchy

The operation of a sugar plantation thus imposed a rigid hierarchy on its slave population. At the top, the boilers and other skilled artisans shared a position of privilege with the drivers who superintended the labour of the fields and who carried a whip as their badge of office instead of a bill or a hoe. These slaves were not only considered the most valuable by their owners, but also enjoyed status among their fellow slaves – something which, ironically perhaps, made them prominent among the leaders of rebellions. Field hands, men and women alike, were categorised by physical strength and traditionally divided into three gangs, with the first, or great gang, responsible for the most onerous tasks, such as digging cane-holes, and the third gang, made up of the elderly and the children, employed in weeding and picking grass as fodder for the estate's livestock. Any field-hand who survived long enough inevitably progressed up from the third gang to the first and back down again, until finally they were so old and infirm that they were listed in estate inventories as 'worthless' and it was considered an act of charity to give them a job as a watchman so that sooner or later they could catch their death of pneumonia and cease to be a burden on the estate. Long after the end of slavery, the frequent reward of a lifetime's agricultural labour was a miserable old age.

It used to be said in Barbados of anyone who looked old before his time, 'he look as if he does dig cane-holes.' Field labour was not only onerous, it had no status. By contrast, domestic service was valued by slaves not only because it meant proximity to the master and his family – and with that, better food and clothing – but because it also kept the domestics, and their children, out of the field. Domestics might pay for their privileges by being more exposed to outbursts of temper and violence on the part of master or mistress, but there was nothing worse than the threat of being sent into the field. As it was customary to exempt the mulatto children of master, manager or overseer from field labour, the plantation stratified jobs not only in terms of status, but also in terms of colour. The lighter the colour of your skin, the better your status and the easier your job, at least in terms of physical work, and this sort of connection has continued to affect social attitudes in many parts of the Caribbean until the present day.

In a debate at an academic conference in 1956, a debate still referred to by Caribbean historians more than forty years later, Eric Williams (then Chief Minister, and later Prime Minister, of Trinidad and Tobago) insisted that:

The distinction between races in the Caribbean area has, for the most part, been a distinction between those who owned property, principally land, and those who worked on it. The racial distinction between European and African before emancipation or between European and Asian after emancipation was fundamentally an economic distinction between the slave-owner and the slave before emancipation and between the planter and indentured immigrant after emancipation. The distinction in race or colour was only the superficial visible symbol of a distinction which in reality was based on the ownership of property.

It is a neat definition, and there is a great deal of truth in it: Williams' argument, developed in his *Capitalism and Slavery* (1944), that the enslavement of Africans in the New World came about purely for economic reasons, has long been generally accepted by historians, unlike the corollary he gave it, that slavery was eventually abolished purely for economic reasons, because it had ceased to pay, a theory which still provokes sometimes heated discussion.

However, at the 1956 debate, the American scholar Frank Tannenbaum remarked that 'it troubles me to have Dr. Williams imply that law and tradition, custom and belief, the very texture that ties the life of man into a society, have no bearing upon human policy while economic interest alone determines human behaviour.' Slavery in the Caribbean might have come about for economic reasons, but any institution which was so widespread and which lasted for so long was bound to have effects far beyond the purely economic sphere, effects which had, as Tannenbaum put it, 'nothing to do with economic determinism and a great deal to do with the way mortals get tied up in their own feelings and prejudices – and a prejudice is of the hardest substance, harder to grind down than a diamond.'

As the Roman historian Tacitus said in another context, it is human nature to hate those whom we have injured. The large-scale importation of Africans into the Caribbean as slaves might have started in the mid-17th century simply because the Sugar Revolution needed labour and it was found to be cheaper to import black slaves than white servants. However, slavery was of so horrible a nature that slave-owners seem to have felt a need to justify it. Some, like the poet James Grainger (c. 1721-1766) wrote as though slavery was an unfortunate necessity, and consoled themselves with the thought that miners in Scotland were worse off than slaves in the Caribbean. Others found it simpler to think of their slaves as less than human, as unfeeling brutes on whom any cruelty might be practised if it was needed to keep them at work. This sort of attitude had been found useful long before African slavery became important; in the 16th century one of Las Casas' opponents, the Spanish writer Juan Ginés de Sepúlveda, had used the suggestion of the ancient Greek philosopher Aristotle, that some men were slaves by nature, to argue that this applied to the Amerindians and that they could therefore legitimately be forced to labour for the benefit of the Spanish.

In a similar fashion, in the early years of English settlement in the Caribbean, the exploitation of white indentured servants seems to have

Woman and grandson, Cuba   *Tony Morrison/South American Pictures*

been made worse by the fact that nearly all landowners were English and Protestant, while a large proportion of the servants were Irish and Catholic – masters found it easy to think of servants as belonging not only to a different race and religion, but as being almost of a different species. Scottish servants fared almost as badly, as even though most of them were Protestants they were still not English. Africans were soon treated in the same way, and as early as 1656 it was claimed that 'the planters of Barbados make no conscience of killing their slaves – dogs and them being in one rank in their opinions.'

However, the African soon came to be worse off in many ways. The difference between black and white proved to be more than a convenient method of spotting runaway slaves, and it came to be assumed, as a group of Barbadian slave-owners put it in 1827, that 'the hand of nature has drawn a mark of distinction between the proprietor of the soil and his dependants.' Almost from the beginning, it was established that, while white servants were bound only for a fixed number of years, enslaved Africans remained slaves for life and their servitude was transmitted to their children. In the early years of the Sugar Revolution it was possible to see white servants and black slaves working side by side in the fields, but this soon became increasingly rare. By the early 18th century, the white servant had ceased to be of any importance in the plantation colonies. From field hand to head boiler, every position on the plantation which involved manual labour, whether skilled or unskilled, was filled by a black slave. By contrast, the

97

whites, from the owner down to the humblest 'book-keeper' (an assistant overseer whose duties had nothing to do with account-books or books of any kind), gave instructions.

This system lasted for a long time: in the older established sugar-colonies, like St. Kitts and Barbados, for the best part of two hundred years. The attitudes and prejudices it created are still with us, 'harder to grind down than a diamond.' The outsider may feel that it was all a very long time ago, that, after all, slavery was abolished in the British Caribbean in 1834. It does not always seem that long ago to the descendants of those who had to live through it. In 1992 the *Barbados Advocate* carried a report of the funeral of a nonagenarian called Matilda Beatrice Blackman, who as a girl had known her great-grandmother Sarah Lemon Harding. Matilda Blackman had been about nine years old in 1911, when her great-grandmother died, reportedly at the age of 116, and her great-grandmother had been a slave who 'recounted horrible tales of the gruesome institution of slavery.' It is little more than yesterday that it was possible to talk to people who had heard accounts of slavery at first hand. Samuel Smith, an Antiguan who died in 1982 at the age of 105, gave eye-witness accounts of how in the 1890s, sixty years after the formal abolition of slavery, some planters still whipped and otherwise physically maltreated their labourers whenever they felt like it, without any fear of legal consequences.

The production of sugar under these conditions established in the minds of Caribbean people a connection between race and status that has proved very difficult to break. Black people worked, while white people gave orders. But from an early date, the distinction between black and white was not as clear-cut as some might have liked it to be. Sexual relations between the races soon produced a group of people of mixed ancestry, and white men who fathered children by black slave women often (though by no means always) freed them and gave them some property, either during their lifetimes, or by their wills. The result was the development of a class of 'free coloured people,' and in the Caribbean – unlike the colonies of the North American mainland – both law and custom gave them a special status. The traditional image of slave society as a pyramid with blacks at the bottom, free coloureds in the middle, and whites at the top, had some truth to it, but oversimplifies the reality. Not all whites were rich, and not all whites were slave-owners – long after white indentureship had ceased to be significant, long after black slavery had been abolished, poor whites were still to be found in the Caribbean's plantation societies, and in some territories (particularly Barbados) they were to be found in considerable numbers.

The British colonies had representative assemblies with considerable powers of local legislation, but only whites who met strict property qualifications had the right to vote, and almost until the end of the slavery period both Jews and Catholics were excluded from the franchise. Not all persons of mixed race were free, and those who were varied greatly in wealth and status. Some owned plantations and large numbers of slaves, but while the Jamaican legislature in the 18th century showed itself willing to grant some specially favoured free coloureds some or all of the privileges of white people, in Barbados all free coloureds were denied the right to testify in a court of law and the right to vote until only a few years before Emancipation. While most blacks were slaves, not all were, but there was no legal distinction between the free black and the free coloured. Sometimes the growth of the free coloureds was seen as a danger to white supremacy, and there were attempts to restrict the amount of property they could own or inherit, but these had only limited success. Most of the time, the free coloureds were seen as providing a valuable buffer between the whites and their slaves, and in spite of the discrimination they faced, in the British colonies the free coloureds generally sided with the whites in the event of a threatened or actual slave revolt.

In different proportions, the same variations in colour and class produced different results in the island of Hispaniola. In the French colony of St.-Domingue, the revolution of 1789 in France provoked what turned into a three-cornered struggle for power between the local whites and their external allies, the black slaves, and the free coloureds, who only here among Caribbean slave societies were sufficiently numerous to hope to achieve power on their own. The independence which the new Republic of Haiti finally won by 1804 looked at first like a black victory.

Nevertheless, Haitian history has been troubled ever since by the fact that the country continues to be divided between a predominantly light-skinned elite and the mass of the population who are almost exclusively black. Haiti's relations with its neighbour, the Dominican Republic, have always suffered from the fact that Haiti conquered and occupied the eastern part of the island for more than twenty years (1822-44). Most of the Dominican Republic's population is of mixed racial origin, but people tend to identify themselves as 'mulatto' rather than black, and this is consciously used as a means of differentiating themselves from the Haitians. Official policy in the Dominican Republic has sometimes endeavoured to claim, against all the evidence, that it is a 'European' country, while the national anthem, with its reference to *Quisqueyanos valientes*, stresses a rather tenuous Amerindian heritage. Haitians continue to be both feared and despised: they are still exploited as low-paid migrant labour, in spite of the notorious massacre of thousands of Haitian workers in the Dominican Republic in 1937 on the orders of the dictator Trujillo. During the 1994 presidential election, one of the leading candidates, José Francisco Peña Gómez, was the victim of a well-orchestrated smear campaign which associated the fact that he was black with the traditional Dominican fear of Haitians.

One enduring consequence of history is the way in which race is seldom regarded as an either/or matter. Race is often a matter of self-definition, or of how one is perceived by others, at least as much as anything to do with biology. At the most obvious level, 'white' and 'black' are far from precise terms. The definition long widely accepted in the United States, that 'black' included any person with any degree of African ancestry and that 'white' meant a person of 'pure' European ancestry has seldom prevailed in the Caribbean without some qualification.

In his *History of Jamaica* (1774), Edward Long claimed that the numerous distinctions of shade named by the Spanish were ignored in that island and that 'the laws permit all, that are above three degrees removed in lineal descent from the Negro ancestor, to vote at elections, and enjoy all the privileges and immunities of his majesty's white subjects of the island.' It was not true in all territories that it was possible in law to move from black to white in three generations, but it was almost invariable that having children with someone lighter in complexion than oneself represented one of the few means of social mobility for people of African descent. While perhaps not as common as it once was, this strategy is by no means unknown today. In small societies where virtually everybody knew everybody else's genealogy, the concept of the 'reputed white' or 'local white' came into being, to label those who were socially accepted as white even though everyone knew they had a black grandmother or great-grandmother. Wealth was a great help in such transitions. Those who did not count as white attached great importance to exact gradations of skin colour, texture of hair and shape of features: if a white skin usually represented high status and a black one the reverse, it seemed logical enough to accord higher status to someone the closer they approximated to the white 'ideal,' especially when the world appeared to work like this in practice. In some Caribbean societies, you do not have to be particularly old to be able to remember the days when the 'clerkesses' (shop assistants) in the leading department stores, and the tellers in the banks were all white or light-skinned, and black staff were only employed as cash-boys or to sweep the floors, or when the teaching staff in the leading secondary schools was predominantly white or light in complexion.

'Shadeism'

A great deal has changed since the 1960s, but old habits die hard; there are still many people who would be quick to resent the slightest suggestion that they were being discriminated against in applying for a job because of their colour, but whose own attitudes to other people are often affected by a consciousness of shade. The outsider may have difficulty in working out exactly what is the difference between persons – all of mixed African and European descent – described as 'clear', 'red', 'yellow', 'light brown', 'brown' or 'light black' but such expressions are normally used with precision, though the terminology itself may vary from one territory to another. Hair which is naturally less than tightly curled is still widely referred to as 'good hair' or 'pretty hair' while hair-straightening products are regarded as essentials by a very large proportion of black Caribbean women and people who actually choose to wear their hair in locks or in a 'natural' style are often treated with irrational hostility. In societies where most people are dark in complexion, most models in TV commercials and print advertisements are still lighter skinned, and skin-bleaching creams continue to find a sale.

The sugar industry's continuing demand for cheap labour after the end of slavery led to further diversification of the Caribbean's racial mix. Workers were brought in under contracts which placed them under the virtually complete control of the sugar estates for several years. Most of them came from India, but other parts of Asia, Europe, the Atlantic islands such as Madeira and the Canaries, even Africans freed from illegal slave-ships, all contributed to the system of indentured labour. There were times when class solidarity proved able to overcome racial barriers in conflicts with employers, and there were ways in which the newcomers were both absorbed into and contributed to a creolised culture in which elements from different parts of the world were fused into something new and distinctively Caribbean. In Trinidad, for example, Hosay, which was originally brought from India as a Shi'ite Muslim festival, soon came to attract participation not only from other Indians, but also from black Trinidadians as well. In general, however, the newcomers were fitted into a system which had since the days of slavery been accustomed to imposing divisions of labour on the basis of preconceived notions about race.

In 19th-century British Guiana, it came to be taken for granted that Indians worked in the cane-fields, whilst blacks dug and maintained the irrigation and drainage canals on the sugar-estates: this fitted in with the stereotype that blacks were better suited to strenuous labour than the Indians, but it also reflected the fact that the Indians could be relied on for the field work because their contracts tied them to the estates, while the blacks would work on the canals when they were wanted because this was better paid

India in the Caribbean: Hosay festival in Jamaica, c.1910

Courtesy of John Gilmore

than field work. Groups of Portuguese were brought in as sugar-workers but moved off the estates as soon as they could; many of them became small shop-keepers, and their somewhat anomalous position was shown by the way in which official censuses in Guyana used to put 'whites' and 'Portuguese' in separate categories. In Jamaica, Trinidad and Guyana, a similar thing happened with Chinese immigrants, and in those countries 'Chinee shop' is widely understood to mean a grocery-store.

Caribbean people can and do mock some of the absurdities which can arise from this sort of thing: there is a well-known and extremely funny short story written by V. S. Naipaul in 1962 called simply 'The Baker's Story,' about a black man who bakes good bread and becomes rich, but only because he gets Chinese to front his business, since no-one in Trinidad at the time would think of buying bread from a black baker. The story satirises some of the other popular assumptions: coconut sellers are Indians, and carpenters and masons are black. But race unfortunately continues to have much wider implications. In both Guyana and Trinidad, much of the Indian population is rural, while blacks are more urbanised; Indians go into trade, while blacks fill civil service positions. In both countries, the main political parties are polarised along racial lines, reflecting a black/Indian divide. Things have improved considerably since the racial violence in Guyana in 1964 which left hundreds dead, but mutual suspicion and hostility between blacks and Indians are still common. Marriage between

102

the two groups is rare, and the usual word for a person of mixed black and Indian origin, 'douglah,' is pejorative, deriving as it does from a Hindi word meaning 'mongrel.' The Jamaican expression 'coolie royal' carries the same sort of connotation.

Race and religion

Race is also associated with other factors, particularly religion. In Curaçao it used to be almost invariable that blacks were Catholic, while whites were Protestant or Jewish; while the immigration of black Protestants from the Eastern Caribbean has changed this picture somewhat in the course of the 20th century, it remains broadly true. In Trinidad, the group of locally-born whites known as French Creoles were not necessarily French in ancestry, but Catholicism was and is an important part of their identity; whites of English origin were usually Anglican. Blacks are usually Christian, and mainly Catholic, while Indians are mainly Hindus, with a significant Muslim minority – those Indians who are Christians are more commonly Presbyterians than Catholics, something which reflects the activities of Canadian Presbyterian missionaries in the late 19th and early 20th centuries. It is still possible to find columnists and letter-writers in the Trinidad newspapers asserting that it is a Christian country, calmly ignoring the beliefs of most of the population, and the fact that the highest national honour is called the Trinity Cross is something at least some non-Christian Trinidadians find hard to accept. In Barbados, while there are many who never enter a place of worship except for weddings or funerals, most of the population are practising Christians; the small Indian minority, on the other hand, is predominantly Muslim, and Islam is generally viewed by the wider Barbadian population with some degree of suspicion and misunderstanding.

History has left the different races of the Caribbean with a degree of mutual suspicion and stereotyped notions of each other's behaviour, in much the same way in which the inhabitants of one island all too often view those of another. It is possible to meet Trinidadians who are apparently convinced that 'all Bajans is bullers' (an abusive term for a male homosexual) or Barbadians who assert that 'St. Lucians does eat cat.' While the inhabitants of some islands are often polyglot, those of some others are resolutely monolingual and sometimes harbour deep suspicion of anyone whose language they cannot understand: 'Them must be cursing me' is a standard reaction. Tolerance for some 'others' does not necessarily mean acceptance of all: for example, it would normally be regarded as unacceptable in present-day Barbados for either blacks or whites to use race as a means of criticising a member of the other group (at least in public), but more overtly racist comments about Indians can appear in the media with little protest from the majority. Race is frequently dragged into issues to which it is irrelevant: when what was interpreted as increasingly authoritarian behaviour on the part of Trinidad and Tobago's prime minister, Basdeo Panday, led to strong criticism from the country's media in 1998, the prime minister defended himself by claiming that the criticism represented a racist attack on him because he was an Indian and the leader of a predominantly Indian party, while the media workers who criticised him were black and some of the financial interests behind the media were white. Nevertheless, what is perhaps remarkable about the Caribbean as a whole is not that race is an often – perhaps ever – present issue, but that a region with such a varied mixture of races and cultures, and such a grim history of racism and ethnic tensions of different kinds, should in the 20th century have seen so little inter-communal strife. It would be unduly simplistic to portray the Caribbean as a paradise of racial harmony, but people of different groups who may not always particularly like each other usually manage at least a grudging tolerance and often much better relations than that. In view of the blood-stained horrors which have afflicted other parts of the world in our time, it is an achievement which deserves respect.

7. Freedom for whom?

On the evening of the 31st of July the baptist chapel was opened for worship, a transparency, with the word FREEDOM, having been placed over the front entrance to the chapel-yard. Of course it was crowded. An hour before midnight, some verses of a dirge, composed for the occasion, were sung by the congregation, who then continued in devotional exercises till within a few minutes of twelve o'clock. After a short silence [the Rev. William] Knibb began to speak. [...] He pointed to the face of the clock, and said, 'The hour is at hand, the monster is dying.' Having heard its first note, he exclaimed, 'The clock is striking;' and having waited for its last note, he cried out, 'The monster is dead: the negro is free.' During these few moments the congregation had been as still as death, and breathless with expectation; but when the last word had been spoken, they simultaneously rose, and broke into a loud and long-continued burst of exultation. 'Never,' says Knibb, [...] 'never did I hear such a sound. The winds of freedom appeared to have been let loose. The very building shook at the strange, yet sacred joy [...]'

The Baptist congregation in Falmouth, Jamaica, commemorate the ending of the Apprenticeship system, 1 August 1838; from John Howard Hinton, *Memoir of William Knibb, Missionary in Jamaica* (2nd edition, London, 1859).

Slave revolt and resistance

In January 1634 a group of Englishmen on their way to establish a settlement in what became Maryland landed in Barbados. The expedition's chronicler, an English Jesuit priest called Andrew White, recorded that just before his party arrived, 'The servants throughout the island had conspired to kill their masters.' The conspirators had planned to seize the first ship which came to the island and use it to escape, but they were betrayed by one of their number who was put off by horror of what they planned. Order was restored by the execution of one of the leaders and, no doubt, by the fact that the free settlers were able to muster a substantial force to maintain their authority – White says his party found eight hundred men in arms the day they arrived.

This was before sugar came to be of any importance and the 'servants' to which White referred were almost certainly European indentured servants and not African slaves. But here, within a few years of the island's settlement, was ample demonstration of the fact that the labourers on whom plantation colonies depended did not always passively accept their lot, and that the rule of plantation owners was only maintained by force or the threat of it.

It soon became clear that slaves, like servants, were likely to run away, and that sometimes they would run away together. In the same way, there were times when they plotted to revolt together, as happened in Barbados in 1655. There were further conspiracies among white servants and their loyalty gave cause for concern in other ways as well: in 1629 some of them betrayed Nevis to the Spanish and in 1689 the same thing happened when St. Kitts was betrayed to the French. As servants became less important, however, slave rebellion became an increasing threat. A major slave rising was planned to take over Barbados in 1675, but was betrayed by a slave who had overheard some of the plotters. There were further conspiracies or rumours of conspiracies in the same island in 1683, 1686, 1692 and 1702. In Jamaica there were six large actual armed slave uprisings between 1673 and 1694 and a number of smaller ones thereafter. Several Caribbean territories experienced significant slave rebellions or threats of rebellion in the course of the 18th century.

Not every slave was a rebel, or even a potential rebel, though modern scholarship has tended to emphasise not only the frequency of actual and planned armed uprisings, but also the many ways in which slaves could assert their own dignity and challenge the system in a less dramatic fashion. Individual acts of murder or even less extreme acts of resistance such as striking a white person almost inevitably brought about swift and barbarous retribution. Some slaves committed suicide, procured abortions, or killed their own children rather than resign themselves or their offspring to spending the rest of their days in servitude. Whites were terrified of slave poisoners, though the general lack of understanding of tropical diseases probably meant that at least some cases suspected of being poisoning were due to natural causes.

Many slaves ran away. Some had every intention of escaping permanently, and a number of communities of successful runaways, known as maroons, came into being, with some of these, in Jamaica and Suriname, surviving as distinct entities to the present day. Other runaways appear to have sought only a temporary respite from their condition and to have returned more or less voluntarily, in spite of the fact they knew punishment was almost certain – though sometimes they succeeded in getting the owner or manager of a neighbouring plantation to secure a pardon for them.

Monument to slave revolt in Haiti

Jason P Howe/South American Pictures

Killing or maiming the plantation's livestock, setting fire to cane-fields (and thus reducing the yield of sugar), go-slows, feigning sickness, playing up to white stereotypes of black stupidity, and singing satirical songs about plantation managers and other authority figures all formed part of the repertoire of resistance.

All of this was an almost inevitable consequence of the way in which the many tilled the land while the few reaped the profits. A Barbados planter claimed that he had never slept more soundly than the night before the 1816 slave rebellion broke out, but most slave-owners must have worried at least some of the time about the possibility of being murdered in their beds. The colonies all had militias made up of whatever white men were able to bear arms, and officered by those of wealth and property – the more land and slaves a planter possessed, the higher he could expect his militia rank to be. Later in the slavery period, the free coloureds were also drafted into the militia. These part-time soldiers were, at least in theory, drilled and exercised with some frequency and prepared to resist foreign invasion, but their main purpose was to suppress slave unrest. Visitors might mock the fondness of militia officers for using their military titles off the parade-ground, and suggest unkindly that they were more accustomed to handling bottle and glass than sword and musket, but superior fire-power generally made up for lack of competence and nearly all slave revolts were quickly suppressed. It did help that at least in the more important colonies the local authorities could often count on the presence of regular military and

107

naval forces from Europe. Nevertheless, as the Caribbean proverb has it, 'what don't happen in a year does happen in a day.' In 1753 the slaves in the Danish colony of St. John (now part of the United States Virgin Islands) rose in rebellion, killed nearly all of the white population and took over the island; the Danes only recovered it with military help from the French in Martinique. Finally, in 1791 the outbreak of another slave rebellion in the French colony of St.-Domingue led to a dozen years of warfare which ended in the establishment of Haiti as an independent state ruled by the ex-slaves.

Haiti was every planter's worst nightmare. It was also an inspiration to slaves elsewhere. The knowledge that a slave revolt could succeed, and that the legality of slavery was being questioned in Europe, encouraged major rebellions in Barbados in 1816, in Guyana in 1823, and in Jamaica in 1831-32. These, as much as anti-slavery agitation in Britain or the fluctuations in the sugar industry, must be given credit for the eventual emancipation of the slaves in the British colonies in 1834. In the Danish colonies the threat of rebellion hastened emancipation in 1848, and when slavery was abolished in French St. Martin in the same year (as in the rest of the French Caribbean) it proved impossible to maintain it in the Dutch part of the island when escape from one side to the other was so easy, though slavery lingered elsewhere in the Dutch Caribbean until 1863.

The leaders of slave revolts and maroon wars are now regarded as national heroes: men like Cuffy in Guyana, Toussaint and Dessalines in Haiti, Bussa in Barbados, Sam Sharpe in Jamaica, and somewhat more shadowy female figures like Jamaica's Nanny of the Maroons and Barbados' Nanny Grig. Nevertheless, the ability of Caribbean people, whether masters, slaves or supposedly free workers, to control or influence their own destinies was always restricted by the realities of international power politics. The sugar islands were pieces of real estate valuable enough to be fought over, and surviving military and naval buildings such as El Morro in Havana, the citadel at Brimstone Hill in St. Kitts (still referred to, at least for the benefit of tourists, as 'the Gibraltar of the West Indies'), and those at Morne Fortune in St. Lucia or Port Royal in Jamaica testify to the enormous sums spent on their defence. Decaying memorials preserve a few of the names of the many thousands of European soldiers and sailors who died in the Caribbean from battle, disease or hurricane, while the bronze figure of Nelson in Barbados and the marble statue of Admiral Lord Rodney costumed as a Roman emperor set in its magnificent neo-classical cupola and colonnade in Spanish Town, Jamaica, testify to the glory which rewarded a few more fortunate commanders – though neither of these can rival the grandiose

Rebel slaves attack Montpelier   *A. Duperley*
Old Works, Jamaica, 1832

monument to Antonio Maceo, one of the heroes of Cuba's struggle for
independence, on the Malecón in Havana.

Conflicts with Europe

European nations maintained fleets and garrisons in the Caribbean for
three reasons: for offence and defence against each other, for protection
against the ever- present threat of slave insurrection, and to keep their own
colonists in order.   In 1651 Lord Willoughby and the parliament of
Barbados issued a declaration against the British parliament, saying 'Shall
we be bound to the Government and Lordship of a Parliament in which we
have no Representatives, or persons chosen by us, for there to propound
and consent to what might be needful to us, as also to oppose and dispute
all what should tend to our disadvantage and harme?   In truth, this would
be a slavery far exceeding all that the English nation hath yet suffered.'

This declaration rose out of the special circumstances of the English
Civil War (Lord Willoughby and his allies were still supporters of the
defeated Royalist cause) and it may be overstating things to suggest that it
was an important precursor of the United States' Declaration of
Independence – as was done in 1966 as Barbados' independence approached.
Nevertheless, from an early date the white colonists came to feel that their
interests and those of their 'mother country' were not necessarily the same.
In the 18th century, the colonists might enjoy considerable influence in the
metropolis – in the British Parliament, both the House of Lords and the

109

Commons contained members who owned property in the Caribbean, and some islands maintained 'colonial agents' (that is, paid lobbyists) in London, and these were sometimes MPs. Even before the slave trade and slavery came under widespread attack, British public opinion sometimes saw the wealth of the Caribbean as a corrupting influence. Samuel Foote's play *The Patron* (1764) has as one of its characters a Member of Parliament called Sir Peter Pepperpot, who bribes his electors with gifts of West India turtle, and the title-character in Richard Cumberland's *The West Indian* (1771) is held up as an example of the effects of having too much money: 'They say he has rum and sugar enough belonging to him, to make all the water in the Thames into punch.'

Sometimes they got their own way. The Molasses Act of 1733, which prohibited American exports to non-British colonies in the Caribbean, and imposed high duties on foreign sugar and molasses, was a prime example of legislation which benefited the British West Indian planter at the expense of both the British consumer and the colonies of the North American mainland.

On the other hand, the metropolitan view of the colonies as resources to be exploited showed itself in the system of 'patent offices' whereby many of the more important jobs in the islands could be allocated to favoured recipients in Britain, who stayed there and took most of the profits, leaving the actual work to be performed in the Caribbean by deputies. Several of the British colonies also suffered from 1663 to 1838 from the 4.5% duty, a tax levied on all exports; this was supposed to defray the expenses of colonial administration, but was simply appropriated by the British government for its own purposes, leaving the colonies to raise other taxes to meet the original intention of the duty.

The local histories written from the point of view of the planter élite record a seemingly endless series of disputes between the colonial legislatures and the governors who embodied imperial authority – whether the point at issue was who should be appointed Clerk of the House of Assembly or the governor's right to fees from marriage licences, it always came down to a question of exactly how power should be distributed between two opposing sides.

The 'representative assemblies' might be representative of only a tiny minority within the total population – indeed, of only a minority within the white population – but their claim to enjoy the same privileges as the House of Commons at Westminster was a claim that the colonies had rights which imperial authority could not override. Unlike the British colonies, the French ones had no parliamentary institutions of their own, but they, too, could make their views felt. In what is known as the 'Guaoulé incident'

Seventeenth century plantation house, Barbados   *John Gilmore*

in 1716, an unpopular governor of Martinique and his assistant were taken by surprise on the morning after a splendid banquet and simply packed on board a ship which was leaving the island. Something which contributed to the outbreak of the Haitian Revolution was the way in which the French Revolution of 1789 precipitated a constitutional crisis among the ruling class in St.-Domingue, with a group of planters forming a General Assembly at Saint-Marc in 1790 which promulgated a constitution for the colony which completely rejected the governor's authority.

By the early 18th century, members of the colonial elites had come to have a sense of their own identity, though it was often an insular identity rather than a Caribbean one: they thought of themselves, not as Englishmen, but as Jamaicans or Barbadians or Antiguans or whatever the case might be. In this they may have been influenced not only by their material interests, but also by the growing sense of a local identity which was being created by their own slaves (see Chapter 10).

There is an obvious resemblance to the way in which an American identity developed in conflict with British imperial pretensions in the northern colonies. When this conflict led to the American War of Independence, the sympathies of many among the Caribbean elites were with the Americans rather than with the British. Yet openly siding with the Americans was never a realistic option for the West Indian planters. Their

111

wealth and position were tied to the export of their sugar and the privileged access to the British market which it enjoyed. The French threat had been eliminated in North America by the Treaty of Paris (1763), but it was still very real in the Caribbean. Most importantly, unlike the situation in North America where the relative numbers of blacks and whites were very different, the West Indian elite depended, in the last resort, on British military power to protect them from the slaves who produced their wealth.

Fine words about how the colonists enjoyed the rights of Englishmen, or about how the Crown might be able to do as it pleased in islands conquered from a foreign power, like Trinidad, but could not interfere in the internal affairs of colonies with their own elected legislatures, like Jamaica or Barbados, always came up against the harsh realities of power. When Britain demanded first the ending of the slave trade, and then the increasing regulation of slavery, and finally the emancipation of the slaves, the planters protested vigorously, but always had in the end to give way.

When the slaves in the British Caribbean colonies were freed on 1 August 1834, some quoted the Psalms to say 'This is the Lord's doing.' Even if we find a more prosaic explanation in the politics of the day, it is difficult not to feel that it was good thing that the British parliament bribed and bullied the West Indian slave-owners into surrendering what they regarded as their rights over their fellow human-beings with the promise of £20 million in compensation and the threat of withholding the money if emancipation was not passed through the local legislatures on terms acceptable to the government in London.

With the benefit of nearly two centuries of hindsight, however, it is possible to see that slavery was ended in a way which served to emphasise the power of the metropolis over the colonies, and that the power which had been used against the slave-owners continued to be used against Caribbean people of all classes.

In the interest of the metropole

It had suited Britain to develop her sugar colonies by permitting the slave trade which provided their labour supply and by offering them a protected market for their produce. By the first half of the 19th century, political and economic orthodoxy had changed. It not only came to be generally accepted that slavery was morally reprehensible, it was also claimed that it was uneconomic (a point still disputed by some modern historians).

Protectionism was denounced with equal fervour. In Britain, the Corn Laws benefited the landowner at the expense of the general public, and the rising group of politicians whose wealth and influence came from trade rather than land denounced them with a powerful combination of sincerity and self-interest. Free trade was pursued as ardently as freedom for the slaves, and the Corn Laws were effectively abolished in 1846. In the same year began the process of equalising the Sugar Duties, and by 1851 foreign sugar could be imported into Britain on the same terms as sugar from British colonies. In vain did British West Indian planters protest that they had been forced to give up slavery while planters in Cuba and Brazil were still able to put slave-grown sugar on the world market at prices below those of 'free sugar' – the interests of British consumers came before those of anybody in the colonies, planter or labourer.

The British government continued to supervise relations between employers and employees in the Caribbean. The Apprenticeship system (1834-1838) which formed a transitional stage between slavery and what was supposed to be complete freedom for the majority of the population, the 'master and servant' acts of local legislatures which kept the balance of power in favour of the former, and the importation of indentured labour from India (1838-1917) were all subject to regulation by the Colonial Office in London, and the more outrageous forms of exploitation were occasionally quashed or prevented by its interference. In general, however, Britain's West Indian colonies were seen as forming a relic of the past, an increasingly irrelevant economic backwater in an empire which was expanding in other parts of the world.

While in the late 18th century the West Indies accounted for about one-fifth of Britain's imports, by the 1850s their share had fallen to one-20th. Britain provided a 'Negro Education Grant' on a fairly generous scale (£30,000 a year for five years from 1835, it was then reduced annually until it ended in 1845) which ensured that most of the children of the ex-slaves received the rudiments of schooling until local governments took over responsibility for the education of the masses. The Anglican Church in the colonies continued to be subsidised by the British taxpayer until the 1870s. Virtually the end of imperial philanthropy until the 20th century (apart from occasional grants or loans following natural disasters), these were seen as measures of social control rather than as ends in themselves. The British government's main concern appears to have been that the Caribbean should give as little trouble as possible.

In practice, this generally meant support for the status quo rather than for the progress of the population as a whole. The fear of 'another Haiti', not any real strategic considerations, kept a significant British military and naval presence in the region throughout the 19th century. When black Jamaicans' widespread dissatisfaction with the continuance of social injustice lead to the violent protest known as the Morant Bay Rebellion in 1865,

British troops were on hand to help the local authorities with a brutal campaign of repression which left nearly 500 dead. The same happened on a much smaller scale in other incidents in other territories, such as the Confederation Riots of 1876 in Barbados. Far from insisting on the extension of colonial franchises which remained much more restricted than in Britain, the Colonial Office sought to make life more convenient for itself by pressuring the old legislative assemblies to vote themselves out of existence and replacing them with nominated councils.

By the end of the century, the 'old representative system' had disappeared except in Barbados, the Bahamas and Bermuda. In British Guiana, a modified version of a constitutional system dating back to the Dutch period, and which gave financial control to the elected representatives of what a later official report described as 'a small oligarchy of planters' until 1891, and then to a wider electorate which was still composed of less than 15% of the adult male population, was retained until 1928. Filled with government officials and members of local elites, the new-style legislatures normally remained extremely conservative, and the descendants of the ex-slaves – and, in turn, the children of the indentured labourers – had to wait a century after Emancipation for the approach of anything resembling a real democracy.

Circumstances differed elsewhere in the region, but the pattern of Caribbean people having only limited control over their own destinies remained the same. Having driven out their old masters and large invasion forces sent by both the British and the French, the Haitians proclaimed their independence in 1804 – after the USA, only the second country in the western hemisphere to secure its freedom from European rule. However, prejudice against the ex-slaves kept the new nation isolated. Although Haiti gave help to both Francisco Miranda and Simón Bolívar in their struggle to liberate Spain's American colonies, Bolívar refused to recognise Haiti's status as an independent nation after his own triumph. Under pressure from Napoleon, the United States forbade trade with Haiti from 1806 to 1809. France continued to have hopes of regaining its former colony, and did not recognise Haitian independence until 1825, and then only in return for an enormous indemnity (150 million francs).

Britain had been quick to secure a substantial share of Haitian trade in the absence of the Americans, and King Henri Christophe (ruler of northern Haiti, 1807-1820) was an admirer of British institutions; nevertheless, Britain did not accord formal recognition until after the French had done so, and trade between Haiti and the British colony of Jamaica was explicitly forbidden by British law. Afraid of what effect the sight of 'mulatto Consuls or black Ambassadors' in American cities might have on their own slaves, the United States refused to recognise Haiti until 1862, although it permitted trade. While the devastation caused by the long war of independence and internal divisions (especially the enduring rivalry between blacks and mulattos) caused their own problems, international isolation and the French indemnity played a large part in retarding Haiti's development. To pay even the first instalment of the indemnity, Haiti had to borrow heavily, establishing a burden of foreign debt and repeated foreign intervention in the country's financial affairs which has persisted until the present.

The struggle for independence

Like Haiti, Cuba fought for its independence. The conflict known as the Ten Years' War which broke out in 1868 promised much, particularly from the way blacks and whites fought together for freedom from the Spanish. On the other hand, the Spanish continued to see Cuba as a valuable possession, and devoted considerable resources in both men and money to maintaining control of the island. The struggle was largely confined to the eastern part of the island, and the rebels finally agreed to terms in 1878. The slaves in the rebel army gained their freedom, and slavery itself was abolished over the period 1880-86 (it had already been abolished in Puerto Rico in 1873). However, promised political reforms which would have given the Cubans more say in their own affairs were never implemented, and a new war for independence broke out in 1895.

Since 1823, the United States had claimed, in the words of President James Monroe, in what would be called the 'Monroe Doctrine' that 'the American continents ... are henceforth not to be considered as subjects for future colonization by any European Power' and that European intervention in the Americas would be regarded as 'the manifestation of an unfriendly disposition towards the US.' For much of the century, the US was preoccupied with its own westward expansion at the expense of Mexico and the Native American peoples and the Monroe Doctrine had little real effect.

While some Americans thought an openly expansionist policy in Central America and the Caribbean was desirable, not all did — before the Civil War (1861-65) the slave-holding States of the South were much more in favour of annexing Cuba than the North — and government policy fluctuated. From time to time there were unsuccessful attempts to secure a naval base in Haiti or the Dominican Republic. Especially in the earlier period, some Cubans were prepared to countenance annexation by their northern neighbour as a means of preserving slavery and the plantation system, and the US government was sometimes prepared to take the idea

US cavalrymen in the Dominican Republic, 1916

seriously – in 1848, for example, it offered to buy Cuba from Spain for $100 million.

By the end of the century, there was an increasing awareness of the strategic significance of the Caribbean to a greatly enlarged US, which by mid-century stretched from Florida to California and looked to the construction of rail or canal routes across Central America to improve communications between its two coasts. In 1895 the US forced Britain to agree to arbitration in its dispute with Venezuela over the British Guiana boundary (a problem that continues to have echoes to the present, with Venezuela claiming about a third of Guyana's territory) and this episode was widely regarded, then and since, as a recognition of the US as the predominant power in the hemisphere. There was considerable backing for the idea that financial as well as strategic considerations justified US intervention in the conflict between Spain and the Cubans, and the blowing up of the US battleship *Maine* in Havana harbour in February 1898 (an event which has never been satisfactorily explained, though it may in fact have been an accident) provided the pretext for a declaration of war.

The US navy swiftly defeated the Spanish in both the Caribbean and the Pacific. Land operations in Cuba took a little longer, and in defeating the Spanish the US military managed to take advantage of the efforts of the Cuban revolutionaries without giving them any credit. The war ended with the Treaty of Paris signed in December 1898: as well as territory in the Pacific, the United States acquired Puerto Rico and a dominant role in a

116

Cuba which became nominally independent. After three years of US military government (1899-1902), what post-1959 Cuban historians refer to as the 'pseudo-republic' came into being, its constitution burdened by the 'Platt Amendment' imposed by the US, with its provision 'That the government of Cuba consents that the United States may exercise the right to intervene for the protection of Cuban independence, the maintenance of a government adequate for the protection of life, property and individual liberty, and for discharging the obligations with respect to Cuba imposed by the treaty of Paris on the United States, now to be assumed by the government of Cuba.' As a North American scholar noted in the 1910 edition of the *Encyclopædia Britannica*, 'The status thus created is very exceptional in the history of international relations.' Other provisions included a restriction on Cuba's right to borrow money, and gave the US the right to buy or lease land for 'coaling or naval stations' – this is the origin of the US naval base at Guantánamo Bay, which still exists, although the Castro government rejects the US claim to it as being based on an unequal treaty.

The United States intervened repeatedly in Cuba's affairs, most notably in 1906-1909, when it stationed troops in the island in support of a provisional government it imposed, and again in 1933, when a show of force – thirty warships cruising up and down in Cuban waters for five months – secured the resignation of a Cuban president who was too radical for American taste. The Platt Amendment was finally abrogated in 1934. It had distorted the development of Cuban politics, and provided the cover for greatly increased US involvement in the island's economy. One other consequence was that American-owned businesses, and the attitudes of US officials and military personnel in the island, fostered an already existing racism, and Afro-Cubans who had fought side by side with whites in the independence struggle found themselves once more relegated to subordinate roles in Cuban society.

8. Towards a Caribbean community

The Caribbean Sea acts both as a barrier and as a bridge. Both functions favour the new internationalization of corruption and violence. By balkanizing the region into relatively weak nation states while at the same time facilitating the flow of international commerce and transnational activities of some of the world's great producers and exporters, this sea puts many an international activity beyond the reach of nation states.

Anthony P. Maingot, *The United States and the Caribbean* (1994)

... an American Secretary of State, Henry Kissinger, proposed to Latin American Foreign Ministers at our 1974 Conference in Tlatelolco a 'Community of the Western Hemisphere.' He had proposed it earlier to Europe in terms of a Community of the North Atlantic and been courteously sent away. It was a memorable encounter in Mexico. Dr Kissinger was told in unequivocal terms that as between unequals 'community' implied hegemony – and we were obliged to ask 'Where, anyway, are Canada and Cuba in this concept of 'Community?' The former he dismissed as an 'add-on'; the latter my colleague from Jamaica, Dudley Thompson, chided him for treating as 'a four-letter word.' Of course, the 'Community' did not happen.

Sir Shridath Ramphal, 'Why the 'C' in the ACP must include Cuba.' (Address to the 8th Europe-Caribbean Conference, Havana, 1997)

Visiting academic: Tell me Sir James, you've occupied many positions in the course of a long career – you've been Minister of Education, now you're Minister of Foreign Affairs – what have you liked best?
Sir James Tudor: Oh, I much preferred being Minister of Education – when you're Minister of Foreign Affairs for a country like Barbados, all you ever get to do is listen.

(One of those unverifiable anecdotes you hear at parties.)

Real estate: the Caribbean and hemispheric interests

Soon after the Spanish-American War, the United States became involved in the building of the Panama Canal (1904-1914), an enormous project which depended not only on American investment and technology, but also on the efforts of thousands of labourers from the Caribbean islands, particularly Jamaica and Barbados. The Canal not only represented an investment of what was then the prodigious sum of $300 million; it was also of immense commercial and strategic significance, and increased the importance to the United States of the Caribbean as a whole. This was emphasised by growing German interest in the region (particularly in Haiti), and by the outbreak of the First World War (1914-1918). The US had supported Panama's separation from Colombia in 1903 and, as well as securing formal control of the Canal Zone 'in perpetuity,' intervened in the country on several occasions in the period 1903-1930.

Internal disturbances in the countries concerned and the desire to protect US strategic and economic interests led to prolonged occupations of both Haiti (1915-1934) and the Dominican Republic (1916-1924), and there were other military interventions in Mexico and Nicaragua. In 1917, what became the United States Virgin Islands were bought from Denmark for $25 million. Even before the USA entered the Second World War (December 1941) it had in September 1940 acquired the right to establish naval bases in several of the British Caribbean colonies, in exchange for supplying Britain with fifty over-age destroyers. By mid-1943 these bases had almost eliminated the threat caused by German submarine attacks in the region, which had caused heavy damage to Allied shipping, including tankers carrying oil from Venezuela and the refineries in Trinidad, Aruba and Curaçao: between January and August 1942, German U-boats sank 59 vessels in the Gulf of Mexico and 220 in the Caribbean.

Another consideration was the presence in Martinique of a large naval force under the command of Admiral Georges Robert, who remained loyal to the German-dominated Vichy regime in France, but who was eventually persuaded to remain neutral and finally pressured by the US into handing over control to a representative of the Free French in July 1943. In Europe the Netherlands were occupied by the Germans, and the Netherlands East Indies were occupied by the Japanese, leaving Suriname and the Netherlands Antilles as the only Dutch territory not under enemy control; in 1941 the United States sent troops to Suriname to protect its bauxite supplies, and in February 1942 took over from the British the occupation of Curaçao and Aruba to protect their oil refineries.

The construction of the US bases provided much needed employment in the British colonies, and directly and indirectly they brought considerable

Pay day for Jamaican workers on the Panama Canal, c1905   *Courtesy of John Gilmore*

sums of money into the local economies. The wages paid by the Americans were often significantly higher than those which had prevailed locally, and in spite of the way in which they brought their own prejudices on the subject of race with them, they did in many cases give local black workers access to positions which they would not have achieved if matters had been left to colonial officials and the local white establishments. Nevertheless, the fact that the agreement concerning the bases had been concluded by Britain and the US without reference to the Caribbean territories involved was resented by a developing Caribbean nationalism and caused problems which were not to be resolved until after independence.

By the time the Second World War broke out, there had been a number of events which hastened the process of social and political change in the British colonies. The series of eventually successful attempts to construct a canal through the Isthmus of Panama had given jobs to thousands of workers from Jamaica and the Eastern Caribbean: from 1850 to 1915 some 174,000 Jamaicans had left their homeland for Panama; 65,000 Barbadians went between 1881 and 1914, as well as smaller but still significant numbers from the rest of the Caribbean. Although digging the 'Great Ditch' was hard and dangerous, it paid better than cutting cane back home and enabled many to save or send money to their relatives – 'Panama money' gave a modest prosperity to many families and in some cases enabled people to meet the property qualifications for the vote for the first time. However, when the Canal opened, there was no longer any work for most of the West Indian labourers and many had to go home, though rather more than half remained in Panama, where their descendants are still to be found.

121

The boom in sugar prices after the First World War created a demand for labour which attracted workers from the British colonies to Cuba and the Dominican Republic. Once again, this proved a temporary phenomenon, but there are parts of Cuba where you might encounter a little girl who speaks no English and whose grandparents moved to the area in the 1920s but who will solemnly assure you 'Soy jamaiquina.' A transplanted version of the 'mummings' (popular street theatre/dances) of St. Kitts and Nevis can be found in San Pedro de Macorís in the Dominican Republic, and there are those who claim that the prowess at baseball which has made Dominicanos so successful in the professional game in the United States (see Chapter 10) is in part attributable to the adaptation of cricketing skills brought by immigrants from the Eastern Caribbean.

Although conscription did not apply in the British colonies, the First World War saw many men join up. This was not an entirely new phenomenon – the British had used West Indian troops in the Ashanti Wars of the 19th century, for example, but it now took place on a large scale. Eleven battalions were recruited as the West India Regiment (1915-1918); the British West Indies Regiment, raised in 1915, was an entirely different unit, and some served in other units, including Canadian and US forces. The Roll of Honour included 142 dead from Barbados alone. For those who returned, the war had considerably widened their experience, sometimes in a very disillusioning fashion. Many of those who had volunteered because they thought they were going to fight for King and Country found that the racial prejudices of British military authorities kept them out of the front lines and that they were treated as little better than labour battalions. It did not help that, after the heroes' welcome, it was often hard to get a job at home and that even when one could be found, pay and conditions were generally poor. Ex-servicemen provided many recruits to organisations like the Trinidad Workingmen's Association, headed from 1923 by a former soldier, Captain Arthur Cipriani, an upper-class Trinidadian who had decided to throw in his lot with 'the barefoot man.'

The Trinidad Workingmen's Association had originally started in 1917, and there were other early unions, like the British Guiana Labour Union and the Jamaica Federation of Labour (both 1919). The legal status of unions in the colonies lagged behind that which they had come to enjoy in Britain by this period, and in the Caribbean they suffered from severe legal restraints. The tradition of worker protest which dated back to slavery had continued throughout the 19th century and into the 20th: for example, Cipriani organised major strike activity in Trinidad and Tobago in 1919, Jamaican railway workers went on strike in 1922, and in 1924 clashes between police and striking workers in British Guiana left twelve dead.

Volunteers leave Antigua for the First World War, c1916   *Courtesy of John Gilmore*

The same period also saw the beginnings of modern political parties, such as the Democratic League organised in Barbados in 1924 by Charles Duncan O'Neal (a friend of Cipriani). Many West Indians were also influenced by the ideas of Pan-Africanism and black self-reliance advocated by Marcus Garvey, who founded the Universal Negro Improvement Association in Jamaica in 1914 and after he moved to the United States in 1916 built it into an international mass movement before his arrest on trumped-up charges of mail fraud in 1922.

However, a general worsening of conditions in the region as a result of the world-wide depression which followed the Wall Street Crash of 1929 led to a series of strikes and popular protests. There were strikes in British Honduras and Trinidad in 1934. The following year there were strikes in British Honduras, British Guiana, Jamaica, St. Kitts, St. Lucia, St. Vincent, and Trinidad; clashes with police in St. Kitts left several of the protesters dead. There were deaths in Trinidad and Barbados in 1937, and in Jamaica in 1938.

In 1938 the British government appointed a commission under the chairmanship of Lord Moyne which spent fifteen months in the Caribbean colonies and produced a lengthy report on their social and political conditions which amounted to a damning indictment of colonial rule. The Moyne Commission's recommendations led to Britain spending large sums

123

in the Caribbean from 1940 onwards under the heading of 'Colonial Development and Welfare' in order to improve social conditions and develop the economies of the different territories. The Commission's political recommendations were much less radical, but the disturbances of the 1930s had encouraged rather than retarded the growth of trade unions and political parties. Local oligarchies and the Colonial Office gave way before steadily increasing pressure and by 1954 all the British Caribbean colonies had achieved universal adult suffrage. Jamaica was the first to get internal self-government, in 1944, and the others followed.

Toward independence: post-war political developments

In 1949 the Jamaican writer V. S. Reid, himself a part of the great flowering of Caribbean creativity which came out of the political struggles of the 1930s, published a novel called *New Day*, in which he praised the constitutional developments of 1944, and linked them with the Morant Bay Rebellion. Many others shared his enthusiasm, and there were many who hoped that political progress in the individual territories would lead to some sort of closer association between them and eventually to their independence as a West Indian nation.

Unfortunately, just as with Morant Bay in 1865, power ultimately remained in the hands of the Colonial Office, and progress was only to take place on their terms. This was shown most dramatically in British Guiana in 1953, where a properly elected government was pushed out of office after only 133 days when the British suspended the constitution and sent in troops because they and the United States feared that that the People's Progressive Party and its leader, Cheddi Jagan, were communists. After the restoration of the constitution, the PPP won elections again in 1957 and 1961; the British response was to allow the opposition a free hand to make the country ungovernable by violent demonstrations, and to change the constitution to allow for voting on a proportional representation system designed to keep Jagan out of office. The PPP still won more of the popular vote and more seats than any other party in the 1964 election; but with backing of the Governor, Jagan's opponent, Forbes Burnham, was able to form a coalition government with the third main political party.

By then, the hoped-for West Indian nation had been stillborn. Ten territories – Antigua, Barbados, Dominica, Grenada, Jamaica, Montserrat, St. Kitts-Nevis-Anguilla, St. Lucia, St. Vincent, and Trinidad and Tobago – came together in 1958 in what was officially called the Federation of the West Indies. This was a culmination of a movement which dated back to the 1930s and which was based on the premise that a united West Indies would be much better able to achieve economic growth and independence than individual territories on their own.   In many ways, however, the Federation was too little, too late. The Federal government had only limited powers, and much was still left in the hands of the governor-general who represented the British government.   While the federal ideal was popular among middle-class intellectuals, it had only limited grass-roots support, and the priorities of many politicians in the unit territories were the interests of their own islands rather than those of the Federation as a whole.   There were disputes over such matters as freedom of movement and the continuance of customs duties within the Federation. The larger territories had enjoyed significant growth since the 1930s and felt that the economic argument for Federation had weakened; instead they were reluctant to, as they saw it, subsidise their poorer neighbours and thought they might be better off on their own.   After a referendum in September 1961, Jamaica left the Federation, and Trinidad and Tobago did the same in January 1962. With its two most wealthy and populous members gone, the Federation collapsed, and it was formally dissolved at midnight on 31 May 1962 – ironically, the date on which it was supposed to have become an independent nation.

The Federal prime minister, Sir Grantley Adams, had practically begged the British to keep the Federation together by force.   This they were understandably unwilling to do, but by this point the British appear to have felt their Caribbean colonies had become more of a burden than anything else and were anxious to get rid of them.   Jamaica and Trinidad and Tobago both became independent in August 1962.   Efforts to salvage anything from the wreck of the Federation proved unavailing.   In 1966, first British Guiana (which changed its name to Guyana) and then Barbados became independent. The following year, several colonies – Antigua, Dominica, Grenada, St. Kitts-Nevis-Anguilla and St. Lucia – became 'associated states,' which meant they got complete internal self-government, with Britain retaining responsibility only for defence and foreign affairs. St. Vincent became an associated state in 1969.   The Bahamas became independent in 1973, and the associated states all moved on to full independence: Grenada (1974), Dominica (1978), St. Lucia (1979), St. Vincent (1979), Antigua (1981 – officially as 'Antigua and Barbuda') and St. Kitts-Nevis (1983).   Belize (formerly British Honduras) had become independent in 1981, and so with the departure of St. Kitts-Nevis, Britain was left with only a handful of colonies in the Caribbean: Anguilla (whose secession from the associated state of St. Kitts-Nevis-Anguilla in 1967 and eventual reversion to colonial status the British were forced, with some

The British flag is lowered,
independence in Jamaica

embarrassment, to accept); the British Virgin Islands, the Cayman Islands, Montserrat, and the Turks and Caicos Islands. (The North Atlantic territory of Bermuda, although similar in many ways, is not geographically in the Caribbean.) All of these have internal self-government, and their colonial status was euphemised into that of 'British Dependent Territories'; in 1998 the British government announced that they would be further restyled as 'British Overseas Territories' and finally agreed (no doubt influenced by Hong Kong's reversion to China and the failure of the spectre of mass immigration into Britain of former colonial subjects to materialise) to grant full British citizenship to all those living in the 'overseas territories.'

The other colonial powers took rather different approaches. In 1946 the French Caribbean colonies of Martinique, Guadeloupe and Guyane voted to become *départements d'outre-mer*, or in other words, to be fully integrated into the French Republic. They were 'overseas departments', but their constitutional position was now exactly the same as La Sarthe or the Alpes-Maritimes, or any other department of mainland France, with their voters sending deputies to the National Assembly in Paris. As part of France, they are part of the European Union, enjoying a protected market access for their sugar, rum and bananas which makes other Caribbean producers envious. The fact that, as French citizens, people from the overseas departments have the right to live and work in metropolitan France, offers an important outlet for migration from territories where economic opportunities are still limited. Whether in the *métropole* or the *départements*

126

d'outre-mer, citizens enjoy the same entitlement to state benefits. There are many other benefits as well, ranging from subsidised freight rates on the national airline to direct infrastructural investment. For some time, a handsome new highway built in Martinique in the 1980s had placards on the lamp-posts displaying an outline map of the island made out of *tricoleur* flags and the slogan, '*Ici l'état investit pour vôtre avenir*'. The sub-text, of course, is that if the locals want independence, they can forget this sort of thing. Nevertheless, while it is generally recognised that the French departments in the region are heavily dependent on the metropole for a highly artificial economy and a standard of living considerably better than that of their independent neighbours, many would like to see rather more local autonomy than the existing regional councils allow within the highly centralised French state system, and support for full independence has grown significantly in recent years.

Having lost their colonial empire in the East Indies, the Dutch agreed to new constitutional arrangements with their remaining territories in the Caribbean. From 1954, Suriname and the Netherlands Antilles gained internal self-government, with Suriname moving to full independence in 1975. There was a long tradition of resentment within the Netherlands Antilles at the dominance of the largest and most populous island, Curaçao, and with some reluctance, the Dutch agreed that the second largest island, Aruba, could leave the Antillean federation and enjoy a 'separate status' from 1986. Aruba was supposed to become fully independent in 1996, but the Dutch were forced to abandon this idea in the face of the increasing reluctance of the Arubans to sever their remaining ties with the Netherlands. The tripartite Kingdom of the Netherlands now consists of the Netherlands in Europe, the Netherlands Antilles, and Aruba; in theory, the three parts enjoy equal status and internal autonomy, leaving certain 'Kingdom matters,' such as citizenship, defence and foreign affairs, to be decided on jointly, though in practice these are dominated by the Dutch. The Antilles were more or less left to themselves for a generation, until a federal political system based on separate island parties, endless coalitions, and short-term policies of keeping the voters happy led to high government deficits, corruption and political cronyism. The Dutch began to take a more active role in their Caribbean territories once more, most notably in 1992, with the imposition of a period of 'higher supervision' on the island government of Sint Maarten. There is some resentment of what is seen as neo-colonialism on the part of the Dutch government, and at the influence of foreign (particularly Dutch) investors and immigrants. In general, however, Antilleans and Arubans seem happy with the continuance of the Dutch connection, which offers relatively generous levels of aid, security for their

127

tourism and offshore business sectors, privileged access to the European Union, and the right to live and work in the European Netherlands.

The 'American paradise': the US in the Caribbean

The United States had in effect acquired Puerto Rico as a colony in 1898 (though the term was never officially used), and Puerto Ricans did not acquire US citizenship until 1917.   This was the same year the United States Virgin Islands were bought from Denmark; their inhabitants had to wait until 1932 for citizenship.   The gradual extension of local autonomy in Puerto Rico led to the change in 1947 from a governor nominated by the US authorities to one elected by the Puerto Ricans themselves.   From 1948 to 1965 the position was held by Luís Muñoz Marín, who was largely responsible for the new constitution for the island accepted by Puerto Rican voters and the US Congress in 1950.   Puerto Rico became a *libre estado asociado*, a 'free associated state' of the United States, and this constitutional situation has continued to the present.   Puerto Ricans are US citizens (and are eligible for drafting into the US armed forces), and are entitled to live and work in the US, but as long as they remain in Puerto Rico they do not pay federal taxes or send voting representatives to the federal legislature. On the other hand, they can claim federal welfare benefits. The US remains responsible for foreign affairs and defence, but the Puerto Ricans have complete local autonomy.

Muñoz Marín used this special relationship to attract considerable investment to the island in the 1950s, the so-called 'Operation Bootstrap.' Puerto Rico benefited from being within the US customs zone, so that products manufactured in the island could enter the US duty free, while US corporations which established plants in Puerto Rico did not have to pay US taxes on profits arising from their operations there.   Essentially, this has remained the basis of the island's economy.   While wages have increased considerably since the 1950s, and Puerto Rico is seen as an oasis of prosperity by most of its Caribbean neighbours, it remains poor by the standards of the US mainland, and its attraction for US investors is still as a reservoir of comparatively cheap labour.   Although the island receives some $10 billion in US aid every year, at $8,000 its per capita income is still only about half that of Mississippi, the poorest state in the USA.

Nevertheless, the US connection is generally regarded as indispensable. Support for independence is very limited, and most Puerto Ricans (in roughly equal numbers) either remain in favour of the status quo, or would prefer to see the island become a State of the USA. In December 1998 the Puerto Rican electorate rejected statehood for the third time since 1967, in a referendum with a turnout of about 71%.   Statehood got 46.5% of the vote, while the other three options (the current status, a modified version of it, and independence) got only 2.8%, but 50.2% of the electorate chose 'none of the above' as recommended by those advocating the continuation of the existing constitutional arrangements, who claimed that the phrasing of the options on the ballot was biased in favour of statehood.

The Puerto Rican situation is true, on a much smaller scale, of the US Virgin Islands, which are heavily dependent on a tourist industry geared largely to the US market. They sell themselves as 'the American Paradise,' where a sunshine holiday is made more appealing by duty free shopping and the fact that everyone speaks English and visitors can pay for everything in US dollars.

The region's independent countries have in many ways found that, once the new flag has been hauled up and the new national anthem sung for the first time, the 'New Day' is not as glorious as was hoped. Major political upheaval in the last half-century has been comparatively limited: the revolution of 1959 in Cuba; the period of turmoil in the Dominican Republic following the assassination of the dictator Trujillo in 1961; two unsuccessful attempts at revolution in Trinidad and Tobago in 1970 and 1990; the revolution in Grenada in 1979 and its collapse in 1983; the military coup in Suriname in 1980, followed by more than a decade of military rule; the overthrow of the Duvalier regime in Haiti in 1986 and of Aristide in 1991.

By the standards of the early 20th century, there has not been much in the way of direct military intervention either. The United States supported the Bay of Pigs invasion of Cuba by a group of Cuban exiles hostile to Castro in 1961, but fear of escalating conflict with the Soviet Union precluded any major action. Following a coup in the Dominican Republic in 1965, the US landed troops and kept the country under its effective control for a year, before handing over to a client regime.

The US was open in its hostility to Maurice Bishop's People's Revolutionary Government in Grenada (1979-83), but Bishop's murder and the bloody fall of the PRG were due to internal squabbling; when the US did intervene in October 1983, it was with the active support of several Caribbean governments and to a rapturous welcome from most Grenadians. The restoration of Aristide as President of Haiti with US military backing in 1994 similarly met with widespread approval. If anything, Caribbean people – including those strongly attached to the idea of national sovereignty – have sometimes questioned why there has not been more external intervention. Trujillo and the Duvaliers were left in power to tyrannise their peoples for decades, and for most of this time enjoyed US support because they were seen as favouring US interests in the region.

129

US soldier, with policemen from St Vincent and Grenada, the Caribbean 'peace-keeping force' on patrol in St Georges, Grenada, 1984

Philip Wolmuth

That Aristide's radicalism made the US reluctant to take earlier action to restore Haiti's first democratically elected president was regarded as obvious by most Caribbean observers. Apart from the cutting off of aid from the Netherlands, the brutal military regime in Suriname was left to its own devices. For more than twenty years, the governments of the Commonwealth Caribbean showed a remarkable reluctance to confront the fact that the People's National Congress regime in Guyana was kept in power by repeated and systematic electoral fraud.

Since independence, most of the smaller territories of the Caribbean have seen regular changes of government at the ballot box. Even in cases where the same party has remained in power for several consecutive terms, incidents of outright electoral fraud are unusual. The basic problem is, rather, that in a small society where the government is one of the largest employers of labour, the party in power always has an advantage. There are innumerable stories about how someone has been victimised for supporting the wrong party, and in small societies victimisation is easy – a single phone-call can ensure than someone's tax-returns are investigated with unusual care, that a bank loan is suddenly called in, that a businessman who submitted the lowest tender nevertheless fails to get a lucrative government contract, or that a civil servant is transferred to an unpopular department. Sometimes the stories are true, sometimes they are not, but

130

the mere fact that such stories are heard and believed is inimical to the proper functioning of a democracy.

In general, however, the inhabitants of much of the Caribbean enjoy relatively high levels of personal and political freedom. The difficulty which the governments they elect have to face is that they are often constrained by circumstances over which they have little control. The Cuban Revolution of 1959 brought about planned and major social upheaval, and many of the country's citizens benefited significantly from the changes which resulted, particularly in the massive expansion of health care and education. Nevertheless, the Cuban Missile Crisis showed the limitations of the Revolution's autonomy – the Cubans had agreed to the Soviet siting of missiles on their soil, but their eventual removal was the result of negotiations between the USA and the USSR from which Cuba was excluded. Cuba found that it had exchanged dependence on the United States for dependence on the USSR, and much of the Revolution's success was in effect paid for by the massive Soviet subsidy which arose out of extremely favourable arrangements which exchanged Cuban sugar for Russian oil. The collapse of the Soviet system brought immediate crisis to the Cuban economy and growing dissatisfaction with the regime. While Cuba struggles to find a solution by encouraging foreign investment in a way which would have been unthinkable before the 1990s, the continuing US embargo hinders its access to international trade.

Bad neighbours: Cuba and the United States

Even before the Spanish-American War, United States interests had considerable investments in Cuba, some US$50 million in 1896. After the war, when Cuba had exchanged Spanish rule for nominal independence and de facto control by the US, American investment increased. In 1901 the United Fruit Company bought more than 175,000 acres, which it cleared and used to establish two sugar-mills. Other major American investment in Cuban sugar-production followed, encouraged by a treaty between Cuba and the US in 1903, which gave Cuban imports into the US a tariff reduction of 20% (making Cuban sugar cheaper than any other to US refiners) in exchange for tariff reductions of 20 to 40% on US products imported into Cuba.

The 'Dance of the Millions' in 1920, which saw a dramatic rise in sugar prices followed by an equally dramatic collapse in a matter of months, ruined many Cuban producers who were bought out by US corporations. While in 1914, 35% of Cuba's sugar came from US-owned mills, in 1926 it was 63%. There was some US divestment during the Great Depression, but the larger properties remained in US hands, so that in 1955 these still accounted for 40% of Cuban sugar production. US investors also controlled large proportions of Cuba's banking system, telephone and electric services and railways. According to the US Department of Commerce, 'Cuba ranked third in Latin America in the value of US direct investments in 1953, outranked only by Venezuela and Brazil.'

By the usual standards of measurement, Cuba in the 1950s was actually one of the more developed countries in Latin America, but the benefits of this were very unevenly distributed. Nearly one in four of the population over the age of ten was illiterate, nearly one in four of the labour force was unemployed. Housing conditions, particularly in rural areas, were appalling: the 1953 census showed that 54% of rural houses had no toilets of any kind, for 85% their only water supply was a river, well or spring. Malnutrition, parasitic infestations and other diseases were common. The country was also burdened with a corrupt government headed by a ruthless dictator, Fulgencio Batista who, after an earlier period in power had returned to the presidency through a coup in 1952, and who enjoyed the backing of the US.

When Fidel Castro returned to Cuba from exile in Mexico in 1956, only twelve of his supporters survived the landing. That he was able to defeat the much larger and better equipped forces of the dictatorship in less than two years was due to the fact that he was able to win widespread support through promising the mass of the population a better life. Castro marched on Havana in December 1958, Batista fled, and on 1 January 1959 the revolution was complete.

The US reaction was at first cool, and then, as Castro introduced increasingly radical measures, openly hostile. An agrarian reform law was introduced in 1959, and in 1960, when Castro arranged to buy most of Cuba's petroleum needs from the Soviet Union, the US Congress cancelled Cuba's sugar quota. Castro's response was a series of nationalisations between August and October 1960 which virtually eliminated US investment in Cuba. On 19 October 1960 the US placed an embargo on virtually all exports to Cuba, and this is still in existence. The effect was to drive Cuba closer to the Soviet Union, allowing the installation of Soviet missiles in the island and precipitating the Cuban Missile Crisis of October 1962.

The Cuban economy came to be heavily dependent on special trading arrangements negotiated with the Soviet Union, and the collapse of the Soviet Union in 1991 caused a prolonged crisis in Cuba, with a 50% decline in the economy between 1989 and 1993. In what appeared to many as a dramatic change in policy, the Cuban government began to permit a limited return to private enterprise, and encouraged foreign investment in a number of sectors, particularly tourism. While there was some growth in the later

1990s, the economy as a whole remained precarious and government control continued to be pervasive.

The Revolution made good its promises in a number of areas. Access to health and educational facilities was enormously improved, illiteracy was virtually eliminated and the general standard of health and housing raised considerably. A planned economy ensured that there were indeed jobs for all and that everybody was adequately fed. Discrimination against blacks and women was abolished, at least in theory, though in at least some respects practice has lagged behind policy: in spite of official efforts to get more women elected, the percentage of women in the National Assembly fell from 33.9% in 1986 to 22.8% in 1993.

However, the system suffered from the usual inefficiencies of planned economies; for many, job satisfaction was low, and an adequate supply of rationed necessities was not enough when there were very few luxuries. The US embargo allowed the government to encourage a siege mentality, and not everybody appreciated being under the constant observation of their local Committee for the Defence of the Revolution. The regime has never been good at tolerating dissent, whether this took the form of political opposition, religious faith or homosexuality. The economic crisis struck at the provision of social services, and even the adequate supply of rationed necessities was no longer always available. Whether further changes in policy will restore confidence in the regime's ability to provide for all remains to be seen.

A major safety valve for the Cuban government has been emigration. Many middle-class Cubans who opposed the Revolution's socialist policies fled in the early 1960s. The Mariel Boatlift (1980) saw some 125,000 leave the country. Another 35,000 left in 1993. A constant trickle of illegal immigration continues, in spite of a 1994 agreement between Cuba and the US under which the US undertook to issue at least 20,000 visas a year to Cubans for legal immigration. However, the Cuban exile community in the United States has come to be a powerful interest group in US politics, ensuring continuing official hostility to Cuba. Recent US legislation has intensified the embargo by threatening sanctions against nationals of third-party countries which trade with Cuba, even though this caused a dispute between the US and the European Union. US officials have sometimes been heavy-handed in their attempts to discourage relations between other Caribbean countries and Cuba, though such efforts have normally been counterproductive. The prolonged US embargo has undoubtedly caused severe problems for Cuba, but it may have actually strengthened the regime over the years, and if the willingness of other countries to invest in a Cuban economic system which is changing (albeit slowly) continues, it may become an irrelevance. As it is, by 1999 some farm-state Republicans in the US Senate were calling for an end to the sanctions policy on the grounds that it hurt US farmers by restricting foreign markets for agricultural produce. While this initiative was defeated by Florida senators mindful of their anti-Castro constituency, it is an argument which is not likely to disappear.

Regional unity and trade

Apart from Guyana, Trinidad and Tobago, and Dominica, which adopted republican constitutions after independence, the former British colonies have all kept the Queen as the official head of state – even Grenada during the period of the People's Revolutionary Government. While this sometimes puzzles extra-regional diplomats, who wonder how a country whose officials continue to swear allegiance to the former colonial monarch can really be independent, this symbolic link with the past is of little practical significance. More important is the fact that most of these countries retain Britain's Judicial Committee of the Privy Council as their highest court of appeal.

For several years, this has been most visible in the way the Privy Council has repeatedly obstructed the desire of Caribbean governments (and a high proportion of the public in Caribbean countries) to resume the hanging of convicted murderers. There is a widespread feeling that a supra-national court does represent a safeguard against the abuse of power in small countries. In 1990, for example, the Privy Council ruled that a law which had been used by the government of Antigua to harass the opposition newspaper *Outlet* and restrict press freedom in that country was unconstitutional.

Nevertheless, many think it is no longer appropriate for this role to be given to a group of elderly British lawyers with little or no personal knowledge of the Caribbean, and that the region has plenty of highly trained and experienced lawyers of its own who would be perfectly capable of staffing such a court. All proposals for the establishment of a Caribbean Court of Appeal have so far, however, failed as a result of the inability of the governments concerned to agree on the details.

Since the acrimonious collapse of the Federation of the West Indies, there has been a change of opinion. Most politicians in the Anglophone Caribbean believe in regional unity, or at least say that they do, most of the time. Putting this idea into practice with any consistency has proved difficult. Even within quite small countries, there are separatist feelings which sometimes strike the outsider as absurd, but which are based on grievances which are very real to those involved. A 1998 referendum in Nevis calling for separation from St. Kitts was lost by only a narrow margin. Barbuda resents the domination of Antigua, and the inhabitants of Carriacou are not overly fond of being ruled from Grenada. There are divergences on foreign policy: some governments (like most of the international community) recognise the People's Republic of China, while others are among the few remaining supporters of the Republic of China on Taiwan. It is difficult to avoid the feeling that the comparatively large sums of money which both Chinas have spent on aid projects in the region has been a deciding factor in these relationships. One or two governments have been quite successful in turning their possession of a vote in international groupings to their own advantage, and indeed remarkably open about it. By virtue of the fact that a few old men in the Grenadines catch one or two blackfish (a small species of whale) every other year or so, the government of St. Vincent has a vote at the International Whaling Council. Consistent support for Japan's pro-whaling policies (even when faced with the threats of environmentalist groups to call for a boycott of Vincentian tourism) has lead to some very visible benefits: the Japanese and Vincentian flags fly side by side in Kingstown at a handsome fish market complex and bus terminal known to the locals as 'Little Tokyo.'

However, this pragmatic approach to international relations has not always been seen when there has been a need to act in concert. On a good many occasions, the region has lost the opportunity to get a representative elected to an influential position in an international body because, rather than agree on a joint candidate, different Caribbean countries have insisted on putting forward their own separate candidates.

The limitations of sovereignty are perhaps at their most obvious when it comes to security questions. Virtually every Caribbean territory has a significant problem with illegal drugs. While there is some support for the legalisation of cannabis – on the grounds that it is a traditional part of popular culture or because of its role as a sacrament in Rastafarianism – this is quite limited, and most people see crack (for some years the most popular hard drug) as simply a dreadful scourge. Most Caribbean territories do not produce significant amounts of cannabis; none are producers of cocaine. These drugs find their way into Caribbean countries because geographical and other factors – location, the presence of numerous isolated spots ideal for air-drops or beach landings, excellent air and sea connections with the rest of the world for both freight and passengers – make them ideal transhipment points for a trade that is fuelled by demand in North America and Europe. It is the fact that teenagers in Miami and Manchester want crack that turns other teenagers into crack-addicts on the back streets of Bridgetown or Port of Spain. The amount of money involved is enormous, and the organisers of the drugs trade are often better armed than the national security forces of many countries.

Drugs are found in a consignment of rice
Royal Navy Picture Desk

It is easy to condemn corruption, but the customs officer or policeman who accepts the equivalent of a month or two's salary for turning his back for a few minutes, or even for persistently failing to see that the neighbourhood drug dealer lives less than two hundred yards from the local police station, knows that the alternative might be a bullet in the head. In some cases, there is evidence of corruption at very high levels. In general however, Caribbean governments are genuinely committed to doing something about the drugs problem, but lack the resources to do so. Every now and again someone is caught at the airport with a few packages of cocaine, or a boatload of ganja is captured as it is being brought in, but most of the time the unemployed youth who lights up a spliff in the wrong place gets a prison sentence, while the 'big-ups' remain at large. There is a Regional Security System to which most English-speaking Caribbean governments belong, and which has proved its usefulness in terms of co-ordinated anti-drugs activities and in providing practical help after natural disasters.

Much of the effort is left, however, to vessels of the United States Coast Guard – carrying a member of the local security forces as a symbolic (and hard fought for) recognition of local sovereignty in territorial waters. Caribbean governments repeatedly make the point that the drugs trade is

136

Drug trafficking in the Caribbean

In 1998 the United Nations International Drugs Control Programme (UNDCP) estimated that 310 metric tonnes of cocaine transited through the Caribbean from South America.

UNDCP also estimate that about 65%, or 65 metric tonnes, of the cocaine arriving in Europe in 1998 transited Caribbean air, land or sea space. An Experts Group from the European Union visited the Caribbean in early 1996 and assessed that the drug problem had become the single greatest threat to the stability, democracy and economic and social development of all countries and territories in the region.

Source: Drugs and International Crime Department, UK Foreign and Commonwealth Office

demand-led, that it is very largely a US problem, and that the US ought to be the one to do something about it. However, it is rather like the ritual calls for foreign aid after a hurricane – this sort of thing may be undignified, but for small countries with limited resources it is difficult to see any practical alternative.

Regional co-operation by governments and non-governmental organisations has produced some tangible results. There are institutions such as the University of the West Indies and the Caribbean News Agency which offer visible and significant benefits to the region as a whole. The same is true of sub-regional groupings like the Organisation of Eastern Caribbean States and the Eastern Caribbean Central Bank. A Caribbean Free Trade Area established in 1968 with just three members (Antigua, Barbados and Guyana) has grown into a Caribbean Community (from 1973) which now includes most of the region's English-speaking territories as well as Haiti and Suriname.

After a slow start, Caricom has come to make a real difference in terms of the promotion of intra-regional trade, though local particularisms and protectionist sentiments still cause problems and Caricom remains much less integrated than the European Union. A major achievement was the organisation – to a large extent as a result of Caribbean initiative – of the African, Caribbean and Pacific (ACP) countries into a more or less united lobbying group which secured important trading concessions from 1975

The *HMS Northumberland* pulls alongside
a ship carrying drugs

Royal Navy Picture Desk

onwards in the successive Lomé Conventions with the European Union. Another regional grouping, the Association of Caribbean States, consisting of Caricom and its Spanish-speaking neighbours, was established with much fanfare in 1994, but has so far offered little in the way of practical consequence.

The region's relations with the United States, its powerful neighbour to the north, have continued to be somewhat ambivalent. Many people in the Caribbean have an admiration for the American way of life, sometimes based purely on the version offered by American television programmes, sometimes as a result of personal knowledge. Many have relatives in the US, and many have visited the country or would like to settle there. Nevertheless, the feeling that the US tends to throw its weight around, and that its friendship is not always disinterested, produces some resentment. There were so many strings attached to the aid proposals of Ronald Reagan's Caribbean Basin Initiative (1983) that it was viewed with widespread cynicism; some found even the terminology offensive, viewing 'basin' as equivalent to 'slop-pail'.

Many have memories long enough to compare the active interest the US showed in the region during the early 1980s, when it saw the presence of the PRG in Grenada and support for leftist parties in other territories as a threat, with what appeared to be sudden indifference after the end of the Cold War and the collapse of the Soviet block. Politicians and businessmen

138

are torn between viewing the North American Free Trade Area (which gives US companies ready access to cheap labour in Mexico) as a threat and wanting to get in on the act. It is pride as much as anything else which has kept the small English-speaking states of the region steadfast in their recognition of Cuba in the face of some often very heavy-handed threats from US politicians, and to view the original signing in 1972 by Barbados, Guyana, Jamaica and Trinidad and Tobago, of a Joint Diplomatic Agreement with Cuba that was effectively to break the hemispheric diplomatic embargo of Cuba in terms of the lighting of 'a candle of courage and principle,' as Sir Shridath Ramphal (Guyana's Foreign Minister at the time) has put it. The generosity with which the United States has provided scholarships and training for many Caribbean people, and given help in terms of money, supplies and personnel at times of natural disaster is recognised and respected. By contrast, the casualness with which the State Department can issue a 'travel advisory' with the potential to blight an island's tourism is seen as baffling. The determination with which the United States has pursued its aim of forcing the European Union to end the special trading arrangements by which the Caribbean enjoys a privileged access to a share of the European market for bananas – a share which is tiny in comparison with that of US-owned multinational corporations, but on which the economies of four countries friendly to the United States depend – is simply incomprehensible.

If the countries of the Caribbean are not forever to be in the dangerous position of 'cockroach at fowlcock party,' they must learn to put the political and diplomatic skills they possess in abundance to more effective use through greater and more consistent co-operation so that they can present a common front to the rest of the world in the pursuit of their common interests. Unfortunately, the readiness with which Caricom's politicians ignored the central recommendations of *Time to Act* – the 1992 report of the West Indian Commission which they had themselves established, and which called for machinery to ensure a very modest level of greater co-ordination and co-operation – suggests that the Caribbean will be plagued by insular divisions for some time to come.

9. Ooman luck deh a dungle ...

Ooman luck deh a dungle, an one day wan fowl wi' kum krach it out fe har.

Jamaican proverb. In her *The Jamaica Handbook of Proverbs* (1993), Vivien Morris-Brown translates this as 'A woman's luck is under the dung heap, and one day, a fowl will come and scratch it out for her' and offers the interpretation 'A woman must never give up hope. Even under the most gloomy circumstances, there is a possibility that she will triumph in the end.'

L'annee passer moen 'tait youn fille
Youn jeune 'ti fille caille mama moen
L'annee-ca la moen c'est youn famme
Moen ka debat pour la vie moen [...]

Translation:

A year ago I was a girl
A young little girl in my mother's house
This year I am a woman
Fighting to make a living for myself [...]

Martiniquan folksong, as quoted in Raymond Quevedo, *Atilla's Kaiso: A short history of Trinidad calypso* (1983). It was being sung in Port of Spain, Trinidad, in the 1890s and remained popular there for many years. The tune was used by Lord Invader (Rupert Grant) as the basis of that of the famous calypso 'Rum and Coca Cola' (1943).

'Equal in their inequality': women under slavery

A glance through almost any newspaper from a Caribbean country, or a quick surf through the many Caribbean newspapers now available on the Internet, soon shows women in positions of prominence. Outside the region, Dame Eugenia Charles, Prime Minister of Dominica from 1980 to 1995 and the Caribbean's first female prime minister, perhaps remains the best known, but several Caribbean countries have or have had woman as heads of government or heads of state. When Dr. Hilda Bynoe (later Dame Hilda) was appointed as the first native-born Governor of Grenada, Carriacou and Petit Martinique in 1968, she became the first female Governor of a Commonwealth country. Even a traditionally strongly macho country like Venezuela in 1999 elected a women, Irene Sáez, as governor of the state of Nueva Esparta (the Caribbean islands of Margarita, Coche and Cubagua), an executive, not a ceremonial, post. Across the region, it is taken for granted that women occupy leading positions in politics, commerce and the professions.

The court reports and the agony columns of the same newspapers, however, reveal often appalling cases of domestic violence, dysfunctional relationships and simple human misery which indicate that while Caribbean women have made enormous progress (particularly during the last fifty years or so), old social habits and attitudes towards gender issues die hard and that real equality between women and men is something not yet achieved. The contrast between the very visible success of some, indeed many, women and the structural inequality which persists is, like many other aspects of Caribbean society, deeply rooted in the region's history.

A modern Caribbean scholar, Eudine Barriteau, has suggested that 'enslaved black women and men ... were equal in their inequality under slavery.' After Emancipation, 'European gender ideologies fed by the enlightenment discourse of Liberalism promoted the notion of the male breadwinner and the dependent housewife. State policies now viewed women's labour as secondary or supplementary.' During slavery, it must be remembered, enslaved black women (that is, most women in the Caribbean at the time) did face specifically gendered forms of oppression, particularly sexual exploitation by those men (both white and black) who were set in positions of authority over them by the system. The same thing happened to East Indian women during the indentureship period. However, under slavery all enslaved persons were regarded primarily as units of labour, irrespective of whether they were male or female.

In the early stages of a territory's development as a sugar-producing plantation colony slave-owners might prefer to import a higher proportion of males. This was perhaps shown most dramatically in the great expansion

Eugenia Charles, Dominica   *Philip Wolmuth*

of the Cuban sugar industry from the late 18th century onwards. To begin
with, it was common for only male slaves to be imported, and attempts by
the government and the Catholic Church to encourage a more balanced
sex ratio for the avoidance of sin were largely ignored. It was the rising
price of male slaves which led some owners to begin to import females,
whereupon they began to discover that women could be made to work just
as hard as men.   Nevertheless, as late as 1865 it was still possible to find
some Cuban sugar-estates with an all-male workforce.

In general, however, as a plantation system matured, there was a tendency
for the ratio of male and female slaves to even out, and then move towards
there being a greater number of females than males. The slave population
at Worthy Park plantation in Jamaica, for example, was 46.8% female in
1784, but by 1834 females were 59.7% of the total.   There was some
distinction in jobs: the operations of the mill and boiling-house were
predominantly carried on by males, and artisans such as coopers, carpenters,
wheel-wrights and blacksmiths were males.   On the other hand, female
seamstresses were more common than male tailors, and female domestics
usually outnumbered males. Nevertheless, the cane field was the reason for
the plantation's existence, and here women and men were assigned their
tasks solely on the basis of physical strength and performed the same work
side by side. At Seawell plantation in Barbados in 1803, there were 20 men
and 34 women in the first gang, that is, the group of adult labourers assigned
the most physically demanding tasks. While head drivers were men, women
were also given supervisory positions in the fields. The third gang, which

143

A popular artistic impression
of Nanny of the Maroons

consisted of young children employed to pick grass as fodder for the estate's
animals and to perform other tasks which were considered comparatively
light, was usually in the charge of a woman who had become too old for
active labour in the first gang. The second gang (male and female teenagers)
might have either a male or a female driver.

Just as there has been over the last two decades or so an increased
recognition of the fact that slaves often did not passively accept their lot,
but engaged in many forms of resistance to the system, so too there has
been a growing interest in the rôles played by women in slave resistance.
Some women were involved in open rebellion, like the legendary 18th-
century figure Nanny of the Maroons, undoubtedly an historical figure
and now officially recognised as a National Heroine of Jamaica, but who
was also credited with supernatural powers, such as being able to catch the
bullets fired at her by British troops in her buttocks and fart them back at
her enemies. On a more mundane but still significant level were the activities
of Nanny Grig, a slave on Simmons' Plantation in Barbados, who was said
by another slave involved in the 1816 rebellion to have told her fellow-
slaves that she had read in the newspapers that they were to be freed and
'that they were all damned fools to work, for that she would not, as freedom
they were sure to get.' Later she reminded them of the Haitian Revolution,
saying that the slaves 'were to be freed on Easter Monday, and the only way
to get it was to fight for it, otherwise they would not get it; and the way
they were to do, was to set fire, as that was the way they did in St. Domingo.'
A modern historian, Hilary Beckles, has seen enslaved black women as
'Natural Rebels', pointing out that they engaged in all the forms of resistance
also used by enslaved men, such as overt violence towards whites, arson

144

and other methods of damaging the master's property, theft, work stoppages, go-slows and running away.

While it was true that pregnancy often aroused little sympathy among owners and overseers, it was also the case that, in the last half-century or so of slavery, owners were increasingly concerned to keep up the numbers of their slaves by natural reproduction: this perhaps gave women more opportunities than men for using real or feigned sickness to get time off work. Planters believed that slave women could control their fertility and that they refused to bear children as a form of resistance; while allowance must be made for the effects of hard work and poor diet on fertility, the large number of abortion-inducing substances known in regional folk medicine suggests that there may have been some truth to this view. In some cases women killed their own children, or those of their masters: their prominence among house slaves gave women greater opportunities than men for covert acts of violence, such as poisoning.

Until slavery was abolished by law, only a small proportion of slaves were ever freed by their owners. Of these, many were freed because as domestics they had given faithful personal, and in many cases, sexual services to their masters. Many others were actually the children of their owners, the fruit of liaisons between white men and black or coloured women which were often prolonged and perhaps willingly accepted or even sought by the women concerned, but which were never relationships between equals. As a result females significantly outnumbered males among those freed: by 2,566 to 1,445 in Jamaica in the period 1817-1829, for example.

Until almost the end of slavery, free coloureds still faced legal disabilities in comparison with whites and, with the rarest of exceptions, they were never considered as social equals. While some free coloureds received occasionally substantial gifts or inheritances in money or landed property from whites who were their fathers and/or former owners, many remained comparatively poor and performed jobs similar to those of slaves (though nearly always in an urban rather than rural environment). Some built on what they had received or what they acquired through their own efforts to prosper in trade.

For free coloured women, opportunities were limited. Some found a living, even a good living, in the hotel and lodging-house trade, which they came to dominate. In at least some cases, this involved the provision of sexual services, either by themselves, or by slave or free coloured women whom they employed. Many became 'housekeepers' (almost invariably a euphemism for sexual partners) to white men. It was a position which brought material security, and even a degree of respectability, but this never amounted to equality. A notorious example was that of Betsey Goodwin, a free coloured woman whom George Poyntz Ricketts, the Jamaican-born governor of Barbados (1794-1800), had brought with him from Tobago as his mistress. She lived with him at his official residence and was believed to possess considerable influence over him; nevertheless, it was unimaginable that she should sit at his dinner-table when there were guests. As a hostile contemporary put it, she 'enjoyed all the privileges of a wife, except the honour of publicly presiding at his table.' Nevertheless, many observers claimed that most free coloured women preferred being a white man's mistress to marriage to a man of their own status: the legal disabilities suffered by free coloured men meant that for free coloured women there were always significant material benefits to having a white partner as a protector. Inevitably this helped to reinforce and perpetuate the complex set of inter-related attitudes to race, class and sexuality which developed out of slavery.

Post-slavery gender relations

With the ending of slavery, women faced new forms of inequality. Among the wealthier classes, an increasing consciousness of respectability constrained by the demands of organised religion meant that almost the only occupations open to them were motherhood and the supervision of a household of (mostly female) domestic servants. Following the pattern established in Europe and imitated by the wives of wealthy whites in the Caribbean, whether they were Catholics in Cuba, Anglicans in Jamaica, or Jews in Curaçao, enforced idleness became a badge of freedom and progress for women of all colours and creeds: mulatto Catholics in Haiti, black Methodists in Barbados or, later, after the ending of indentureship, Indian Muslims and Hindus in Trinidad and Guyana.

The wives of ministers of religion were permitted to help with their church's social and educational work – often, indeed, expected to do so without any financial reward. Upper-class women might organise charitable events or elaborate social occasions to help further their husbands' careers. For the less well off, for a long time almost the only respectable occupation for middle-class women was teaching, and then only so long as they remained unmarried. No married woman could get or keep a civil service job in Jamaica before 1942. Legislation passed in Trinidad and Tobago in 1919 required female teachers to resign on marriage; this was enforced until about 1946 and not formally revoked until the 1960s. The assumption that married women had no place in the world of employment because they would be provided for by their husbands was widespread and continued to receive official sanction in parts of the Caribbean until very recently. In the Netherlands Antilles, married women were ineligible for permanent

146

Haitian market woman, c.1940
Courtesy of John Gilmore

civil service appointments, and could only be appointed on a temporary basis if there was no man or unmarried woman available to fill the post. This remained the case until 1983 and only in 1994, after repeated strikes and industrial disputes, was another law passed providing for equal pay for all female public servants – until then a married woman received 25% less than a man or an unmarried woman doing the same job.

Most women of course had no option but to work in some form or other. Where the end of slavery led to a decline in the plantation system and a growth in smaller-scale peasant agriculture (for example, in Haiti, Jamaica and the Windward Islands) many women worked on the land, sometimes as independent proprietors, often as free labour for their male partners. Among some of the Suriname Maroons, it is acceptable for a man to have as many wives as he is prepared to clear food-plots for. The fact that clearing plots in the forest is hard work persuades most men that one or two wives are enough, but once the clearing is done he can concentrate on the supposedly more skilled tasks of hunting and fishing which are performed by males, and leave his wives to get on with the routine labours of cooking, cleaning and cultivating rice and cassava which he would consider beneath him.

In a similar fashion, a male Haitian peasant might have more than one *femme-jardin* ('garden-woman') to look after farming plots in different parts of the countryside. There is an economic aspect to polygamous habits: the Caribbean man who visits his 'outside woman' is not there just to demand sex; he expects to be fed as well. The man will normally be providing cash or kind to support his wife (or a 'staunch woman' with whom he has a more or less permanent but not legally formalised relationship) as well as one or two outside women (with whom he may also be involved on a long-term basis). However, he will not expect to be the sole provider: each of the women will also be contributing to the set-up, through earnings from paid employment or some sort of commercial activity such as needleworking or huckstering (small-scale retailing), or (less commonly nowadays) by working a piece of land. It is only the rich man who can maintain a 'keep-miss' in idleness. While there are always men who will take whatever else they can get as well, this sort of stable polygamous arrangement is certainly not promiscuous, even if it is traditionally denounced as such by religious leaders. It is essentially a survival strategy which benefits all concerned, though it often seems that the male reaps an undue share of the benefits. While some aspects of it can be traced back to slavery, it probably evolved as a means of coping with the fact that Emancipation thrust the newly freed into a developing free-market system but left most of the capital and most of the power in other hands. Its continuance is a reflection of the fact that, even in more developed Caribbean countries, the increased prosperity of recent decades has not been spread evenly through the population, and that women make up a disproportionate number of the low-paid and unemployed. Although formal marriage was accepted as an ideal, for most woman and men it was regarded as a luxury which they could not afford. Even now, the traditional pattern whereby couples marry when they are older, after their relationship has already existed for several years and produced children, still survives to a more limited extent.

Some women migrated in search of adventure or simply a better living. Mary Seacole, a mixed-race Jamaican woman who published her autobiography in 1857, probably went further than most: she had already travelled extensively before she spent some two years hotel and restaurant keeping in the Isthmus of Panama. She then took herself, at her own expense and in the face of indifference or hostility of the British authorities, to the Crimean War, where she spent the duration providing good food and medical attention to the British troops fighting the Russians. Her nursing skills were derived not from formal medical education, but from 'Creole medical art' she had learnt from her mother. Official army catering and medical services were appallingly badly organised, and many British soldiers of all ranks provided testimonials that Mrs. Seacole's cooking, nursing and home remedies had saved their lives. Although the sudden ending of the war proved a financial disaster for her, influential friends she had won in the Crimea rescued her from bankruptcy, and when she died in 1881 she was comparatively wealthy.

148

Mary Seacole's hotel in the Crimea, frontispiece in the *Wonderful Adventures of Mrs Seacole in Many Lands*

Courtesy of John Gilmore

Many other women probably shared what Mrs. Seacole called her 'disposition to roam' but comparatively few would have been able to do much about it. While the Panama Canal was by far the most important, in the 19th and early 20th centuries, there were various opportunities for migrant labour from the Caribbean, such as working on ships, building railways in Brazil, or collecting rubber in the Peruvian Amazon. However, companies which recruited labour in the Caribbean and, all importantly, provided passages for recruits, were interested mainly or exclusively in male workers. In this period only a minority of working-class Caribbean people, male or female, could afford to pay their own way to another country, no matter how attractive the opportunities might seem. In the later 20th century, migration was still, at least to begin with, predominantly male. The world of the West Indian immigrants in Sam Selvon's classic novel *The Lonely Londoners* (1956) is almost exclusively male. Some migration schemes, like the seasonal recruitment of labourers to work on farms in the United States (which still continues), were open only to men. Others targeted women, such as the way in which Britain recruited nursing staff from the Caribbean in the 1950s and 1960s or women from some British Caribbean colonies were allowed to enter Canada to work as maids in the same period. Generally, however, the pattern was that men went first and women followed later.

The same thing tended to happen with internal migration from country to town, though here it was often possible for a woman simply to walk to the nearest town or her island's capital and seek to survive as best she could. This often meant being a 'shop-girl' or a maid, at best working long hours for little pay, and at worst being subjected to physical or sexual abuse and obliged to put up with belittling restrictions on her personal life. In his story 'When I Pounded the Pavement' (1932), which draws on his own experiences in the Jamaica Constabulary in the early years of the century, Claude McKay tells how – with the full sanction of the law – the couple who employ her bring a policeman with them to intrude on the maid's room where she is sleeping with her boyfriend and arrest him. He was there with the maid's consent but without that of her employers: the Vagrancy Act had recently been amended to make this an offence, and McKay tells us the man was sentenced to six months in prison and a flogging. He says nothing about the maid's fate, but we can assume she lost her job.

One consequence of migration and of the prevalence of polygamous and 'visiting' relationships was that often women were literally left holding the baby. Sometimes men sent money home to support those they had left behind, sometimes they didn't. There is a folk song widely known in the Anglophone Caribbean in which the man advises the 'brown-skin gal' to 'stay home and mind baby' because he is 'going away on a sailing boat.' It was sung in 1944 by the Trinidadian calypsonian King Radio (Norman Span) as a criticism of the behaviour of American servicemen in the island, and it may have been he who introduced the line about how if the man doesn't come back, as far as he is concerned, the woman can 'trow way de damn baby' (that is, get an abortion). However, the song is usually regarded as a comment on male behaviour in general. There were many households in which it was a case of 'My Mother Who Fathered Me,' in the words of Edith Clarke's classic sociological study (1957) of three Jamaican communities. If the mother followed the father from country to town or overseas, children might be left behind in the care of a grandparent (usually a grandmother) until the parents were ready to send for them. In any case, women had to 'cut and contrive' as best they could in order to support themselves and their children. All too often the only jobs open to them were intermittent and badly paid and they had to turn to the traditional forms of female self-employment: needle-working, doing the laundry of the better-off, small-scale processing of food-stuffs, and the petty retailing which goes under different names in different parts of the Caribbean (hawking, huckstering, higglering) but which is much the same all over the region. All too often a woman who had been abandoned by her children's father sought emotional and material support by entering a relationship

150

with another man, only for this, too, to prove impermanent. The way in which grinding poverty did not make for stable relationships was summed up with brutal frankness in the famous Trinidadian calypso 'No Money, No Love' by The Mighty Sparrow.

We can't love without money
We can't make love on hungry belly
Johnny, you'll be the only one I am dreaming of
You're my turtle dove
But – no money, no love.

The Mighty Sparrow (Slinger Francisco), 'No Money, No Love'

Misogyny in popular culture

At some times and places, men had a certain scarcity value. So many men left Barbados to work on the Panama Canal that the 1921 Barbadian census showed females outnumbering males by at least 20% in every age group from 15 to 69; among those aged 30 to 39, females outnumbered males by nearly three to one. Helped by later migration, a considerable imbalance persisted for decades.

When they could find work, men who stayed at home could expect to be better paid than women and took it for granted that their contribution gave them the right not only to govern the household, but to have the best of everything, if necessary, at the expense of their wives and children. In a song popular in Barbados in the 1960s, DaCosta Allamby portrayed a man who told his woman to 'Endorse de coucou and put it back in de pot' – in other words, take food off the plates of children he felt did not deserve it: 'Dem children don't work nowhere/And I ain't standin' for dat.' On the other hand, she must give him 'a bigger share' for 'I want you to understand/ Dat I am de boss in here.' Women who stood up for themselves or their children, or whose men thought they had cause for jealousy, were likely to meet a violent reaction: in Sparrow's 'No money, no love,' Johnny's response to Ivy's intended departure is to 'nearly kill she with blows'. Ivy gave as good as she got, but if many men saw nothing wrong in using domestic violence to reinforce their authority or vent their frustrations, many women felt that it was a price they had to pay for security – a case of 'Eat soldier food, tek soldier blows' as the proverb puts it. Attitudes appear to be changing and an increase in the number of cases of domestic violence reported to the police in several Caribbean territories may reflect a greater willingness on the part of women to complain rather than an actual increase

151

in this type of crime. Nevertheless, it remains the case that male violence against women is not uncommonly regarded as something which is only to be expected, even if it is not actually condoned.

'Endorse de coucou' is just one example of misogyny in popular culture. Women are portrayed as willing to go to any lengths to get a man. In the Barbadian folk-song 'Da Cocoa-Tea' (possibly dating back to the late 19th century) the male singer complains about the woman who has used a love potion to secure his affections and poisoned him in the process: 'she got muh head upsided down/Wid a cup o' da cocoa-tea.' In 'Obeah Wedding' (1966) Sparrow tells a woman she is 'only wasting time' trying to use magic to get him to marry her, for she would do better to pay more attention to her personal hygiene if she wants somebody to marry her. The Roaring Lion (Rafael de Leon) claimed in 'Ugly Woman' (1933), that the man who marries a pretty woman will always have cause for jealousy: 'when you think that she's belonging to you/She calling somebody else doudoudou [darling]/Therefore from a logical point of view/Should always love a woman uglier than you.' Invader's 'Rum and Coca Cola' (1943) with its 'Both mothers and daughters/Working for the Yankee dollar' is not about the things women have to do to survive, but about sexual rivalry between white American service personnel and the black Trinidadian men who could not compete with them financially: 'the young girls [...] said that the Yankees treat them nice/And they give them a better price.'

Sparrow's 'Jean and Dinah', first sung in 1956 and still popular, celebrates the closure of the US naval base in Trinidad in specifically sexual terms. With the Americans gone, the local men will 'have things back in control' but it is made clear that the 'things' the singer has in mind are 'the girls in town.' Sparrow is 'seeking revenge with me heart and soul' and the male triumphalism of 'Yankees gone, Sparrow tek over now' expresses itself in the degradation of women:

> It's the glamour boys again
> We are going to rule Port of Spain
> No more Yankees to spoil the fête
> Dorothy have to take what she get [...]

While songs like 'Da Cocoa-Tea' or Roaring Lion's 'Concertina' (late 1950s), with its string of double entendres about a sexually voracious woman, express male insecurities, many others urge female compliance with male sexual demands. Some of the most notorious examples are Jamaican, from Max Romeo's international hit 'Wet Dream' (1969), with its insistent 'Lie down gal, lemme push it up, push it up' through to Admiral

152

Bailey's 'Want Punnanny' (1987) and onwards. Female compliance is, if necessary, secured by male violence, a theme found the length and breadth of the Caribbean, from the Trinidadian calypso 'Turn Them Down' (dating back at least to the 1940s but popularised once more by Sparrow in the 1970s) with its 'Black up dey eye and bruise dey knee/And then dey love you eternally', to the Puerto Rican salsa 'Bandolera' (1978) in which Héctor Lavoe sings 'te voy a dar una pela/pa' que aprendas a querer' ('I'm going to hit you so you may learn to love'). A folk-song like 'Murder in de Market' (apparently based on a real incident in Barbados in the 1870s, though there is a later, Trinidadian version) refers to a woman who 'ain't kill nobody but she husband' and accordingly seems to feel that she has nothing to fear: 'she facin' de judge independent.'

But there are also songs like 'Millie gone to Brazil/Oh Lawd poor Millie' about a case in the 1920s in which a Barbadian claimed that his missing wife had gone to Brazil when in fact he had murdered her and dumped her body down a well. What is significant is not so much the original song as the way in which it has come to be preserved as a picturesque piece of local folk-lore and choirs sing of 'poor Millie/Wid de wiah [wire] tie up she wais'/An de razor cut up she face' with gleeful enthusiasm. There are a few widely known female performers, like Cuba's Celia Cruz, and others who are popular in their own territories and their expatriate communities (if little known elsewhere, even among other Caribbean groups), like Dominica's Ophelia. However, the voices of Caribbean popular culture, certainly of Caribbean popular music, are predominantly male, and there are not many like Trinidad's Singing Sandra, who had a hit in the 1980s telling an unwanted man 'You can keep your money/I'll keep my honey/ And die with my dignity.'

Popular attitudes were long reinforced by various forms of legal discrimination. Of these, the most important was the right to vote. While in most Caribbean territories the franchise was restricted to a comparatively small part of the population until the mid-20th century, it was long the case that out of those who could vote, all were men. In Barbados women only got the vote in 1943, at a time when the franchise when still restricted by property qualifications; only from 1950 were all adult women and men entitled to vote. In Haiti women got the vote in 1950, but until 1982 Haitian married women were still legally regarded as minors, and even then the legal abolition of this status only affected women who married subsequently.

The present low status of women in the West Indies makes it the more important to secure essential equality of educational opportunity between the sexes. If there are to be happy marriages girls must be able to be companions to their husbands and therefore need every opportunity for as wide a cultural education as possible. In the early age-groups, there is no marked difference between boys and girls as regards school attendance; but in the older classes the numbers of girls fall off, partly because girls are kept at home to look after the younger children. This falling off is very marked among East Indians, but is perceptible throughout [...]

In the matter of secondary education, girls are at a disadvantage as compared with boys. The number of girls enrolled in secondary schools is generally (though not universally) well below that of boys; and it must be borne in mind that these figures include those for preparatory sections to which small boys are admitted. Government provision for girls' secondary education is much lower than for boys; there is no Government Secondary School for Girls in British Guiana or Trinidad and only one (St. Vincent) in the whole of the Windwards and Leewards.

West India Royal Commission Report (the Moyne Report; published 1945), describing conditions in British Caribbean colonies immediately before the Second World War.

New roles for women

Educational provision varied greatly from one Caribbean territory to another, but until the second half of the 20th century, girls generally had less access to whatever was available than boys. In Haiti in 1938, only 10% of all children went to school at all, and girls accounted for less than one in three of pupils attending state-run rural schools. In other territories in the same period, many children spent much of their time, not in school, but engaged in agricultural labour to help support their families. In the British colonies, while boys and girls had more or less equal access to primary education, secondary education was not only restricted to a minority but also made much less provision for girls than for boys.

The period after the Second World War saw the beginning of widespread change. Governments systematically made more comprehensive provision for the education of girls, and although past neglect continued to have its effects, patterns of achievement began to change in younger generations.

154

Women working in US-owned lingerie factory, St. Lucia   *Philip Wolmuth*

In Trinidad and Tobago in 1965, there were five times as many men as women among people with a university education; by 1971 the proportion was four to one.   In the Anglophone Caribbean in more recent decades it is frequently suggested that the situation has virtually reversed itself, and that while women are successfully making use of the educational opportunities available to them, men are failing to achieve and falling behind.

Critics point to statistics like the fact that women have for some time been a significant majority among students at the Cave Hill (Barbados) campus of the University of the West Indies (currently around 70%) and it is claimed that the widespread adoption of coeducation in schools and the greatly increased number of female teachers disadvantages male pupils. This is often hotly debated, but the levels of educational underachievement, unemployment and criminality among male youths which give genuine cause for concern perhaps need to be attributed to wider structural problems in society and not solely to changes in the educational system.

In the second half of the 20th century, Caribbean women built on the power they had acquired as voters and on their improved access to education, to become more prominent in public life and in a much wider range of occupations.   For example, Rose Leon (died 1999) first became a member of the Jamaica House of Representatives in 1949 and was Minister of Health and Housing from 1953 to 1955 as well as serving as chairman of the

Jamaica Labour Party from 1945 to 1965. After falling out with the JLP, she joined the People's National Party and was Minister of Local Government in the PNP government from 1972 to 1976. Dominica's Phyllis Shand Allfrey (1908-1986) was not only an important writer and journalist (best known as author of the novel, *The Orchid House*, 1953), but also one of the founders of the Dominica Labour Party and Minister of Labour and Social Affairs in the federal government during the Federation of the West Indies (1958-1962). More grimly, in the Dominican Republic the three Mirabal sisters became national heroines by being murdered for their opposition to the dictatorship of Trujillo.

Many women have also achieved success in business, the professions (including law and medicine, traditionally two of the occupations with the highest status in much of the region) and government administration. By the end of the century, in most Caribbean territories the presence of women in traditionally male occupations is scarcely matter for comment, even if in some areas, such as the military, they still often (though not invariably) find themselves in conventionally female roles like health care and secretarial duties. Women have long been prominent in some Caribbean churches from the Hart sisters (Methodist and anti-slavery activists in Antigua in the late 18th century) onwards, but it was generally only indigenous Afro-Christian groups which offered them leadership positions. While the Catholic church remains all-male in its leaders, in recent years ministerial functions in other 'mainstream' churches have frequently come to be performed by women. In August 1999, for example, a bishop of the Anglican (Episcopalian) Church in Jamaica commented on a service at which he had just ordained two priests and seven deacons, 'Who would have thought two years ago that we would have had the ordination of nine ordinands in which there is only one male and eight females?' (While some Anglican churches elsewhere now have women as bishops, however, this is not yet the case in the Caribbean.) The contribution of women to many areas of modern Caribbean culture is enormous; any brief list can do no more than give a few examples, such as Cuba's Alicia Alonso and Trinidad's Beryl McBurnie in dance, Jamaica's Louise Bennett and Barbados' Daphne Joseph-Hackett in theatre, Antigua's Jamaica Kincaid, Dominica's Jean Rhys, Grenada's Merle Collins, Guadeloupe's Maryse Condé and Jamaica's Olive Senior in literature, and Jamaica's Edna Manley in the visual arts.

The struggles which it cost me to succeed in life were sometimes very trying; nor have they ended yet ... Although it was no easy thing for a widow to make ends meet, I never allowed myself to know what repining or depression was, and so succeeded in gaining not only my daily bread, but many comforts besides, from the beginning.

Mary Seacole, *Wonderful Adventures of Mrs. Seacole in Many Lands*, 1857

Women seem to have great freedom in Caribbean societies, yet we know that women suffer great inequalities within them.

Carole Boyce Davies and Elaine Savory Fido, introduction to *Out of the Kumbla: Caribbean Women and Literature* (1990)

Challenges ahead

However, in spite of the undoubted achievements of those in high-profile positions, it is still the case that while for Caribbean women in general there has been great progress, many problems remain. Women still remain under-represented in the political process: in Puerto Rico in 1996, for example, women were 53% of voters but made up only 18% of the membership of the legislature. Women who do run for political office still face abuse from public platforms from male (and occasionally female) opponents who seek to exploit the persistence of traditional gender stereotypes among voters. The more blatant forms of legal discrimination have been abolished, though some persist: in a number of Caribbean territories it remains the case that while the children of a male citizen by a woman who is a foreign national have a right to citizenship the reverse is not the case.

In the 1970s and 1980s a whole series of reforms in different Caribbean countries modernised legislation relating to marriage and the family. One important consequence was the virtual abolition of the concept of illegitimacy. Traditional patterns of relationships meant that a high proportion of children were born out of wedlock, and a decline in church influence is perhaps the reason for the increase of this proportion over time. In Barbados in 1850, 55% of all children baptised in the Anglican church (which at the time represented some 90% of the total population) were born out of wedlock; in 1980 civil registrations showed 73.3% of all

Women market traders, St Lucia   *Philip Wolmuth*

births as out of wedlock.   In Jamaica, births out of wedlock rose from 60% in 1886 to 85% in 1986.   Such children not only faced some degree of social stigma, but also practical disadvantages.   Scholarships from primary to secondary schools, for example, were often open only to children who could produce proof of legitimate birth.   It was usual for children born out of wedlock to have fewer rights when it came to inheriting property.   Legal changes to ensure that all children have equal rights of inheritance, irrespective of the marital status of their parents, have led to greater fairness.

In other cases, however, legislation has failed to live up to the intentions of its framers.   A recent study of the Jamaican reforms of the 1970s suggested that they were based on an ideology which favoured the concept of the nuclear family in a manner which was at variance with the realities of Jamaican society, and that legislation which was designed to give equal rights to both parents and to encourage fathers to take greater responsibility for their children was actually counter-productive in some cases.   If women were given the right to demand greater financial support from the fathers of their children, fathers also received access and custody rights.   This meant, for example, that fathers were enabled to use the threat of a custody dispute to dissuade mothers from claiming child support to which they were legally entitled.   The experience of other territories also shows that even when a mother does obtain a court order for 'child money', getting the father to pay up can be a problem.

158

Women also remain over-represented among the unemployed and under-employed. Official figures for Jamaica put the unemployment rate for April 1999 at 15.8%, but for males it was 9.9% and for females 22.7%. Barbados figures for the period October to December 1998 gave the unemployment rate as 7.8%, with that for males being 6% and for females 9.5%. While economic development has greatly increased the opportunities for employment across the region since the 1950s, where women are concerned, many of these opportunities are in areas like the hotel industry, light manufacturing and assembly industries and data processing, in which women continue to be used mainly as cheap labour.

In order to make ends meet, many women combine paid employment with some other form of economic activity (as well as having to devote time to housework and other domestic responsibilities). Traditional small enterprises survive, and have sometimes taken on new forms. The old-time higgler still sits by the side of the road with her wooden tray full of vegetables, but international higglering has been around at least since the early 19th century, when Mary Seacole went to London with 'a large stock of West Indian preserves and pickles for sale' or visited the Bahamas and bought 'a large collection of handsome shells and rare shell-work' which she sold successfully in Jamaica.

The modern 'suitcase trader' or 'informal importer' is usually female, and travels by plane to shop in Miami, San Juan or Caracas, or the free zones of Panama or Curaçao. Returning home with a wide range of clothing and other items, she will often succeed in avoiding payment of duty on some or all of them, and is thus enabled to sell them comparatively cheaply to her friends and acquaintances and still make a profit. In some cases she does this more or less full-time, but as a shopping trip need take no more than a weekend, it is possible to combine this sort of activity with more formal employment. The suitcase trader makes a living, and her clients are able to buy items which are otherwise unobtainable locally, or priced out of their reach as a result of the dependence of Caribbean governments on import duties or sales taxes for a high proportion of their revenue.

While a woman may well also be receiving some form of support from a male partner, a significant part of female economic activity (whether self-employment or working for others) depends on traditional support systems which are largely female. While not as universal as it once was, the multigenerational household is still more common in the Caribbean than it is in North America or western Europe. In order to work (especially in somewhere like a hotel or a data-processing plant which operates a shift system), many women depend on being able to leave their children with their own mothers or some other close female relative. Government social security systems exist, but provide only limited assistance: the family still plays an important part in cushioning the burden of sickness and unemployment. Some apparently liberal social measures are open to more than one interpretation. Barbados, for example, has a fairly generous provision of government-run day-nurseries which provide reliable child-care at subsidised rates. Many voters are working single mothers and they have come to expect this sort of provision. While it enables many women to work who would otherwise have difficulty in doing so, it can also be seen as enabling them to work for lower wages and as helping to ensure the continued existence of a large pool of cheap labour. In effect, both this sort of government provision and the extended family mean that the taxpayer in general, and the work (both paid and unpaid) of women in particular, subsidise the development process as a whole, including the profits of employers and foreign investors.

10. Creolising the world?

Creole. – Anything living, born in the West Indies, is called a '*Creole*,' e.g. 'The *Creole* Handicap open to all horses born in the colony.'

Rev. Greville John Chester, *Transatlantic Sketches* (London, 1869)

... mongrel as I am, something prickles in me when I see the word Ashanti as with the word Warwickshire, both separately intimating my grandfathers' roots, both baptising this neither proud nor ashamed bastard, this hybrid, this West Indian.

Derek Walcott, 'What the Twilight Says: An Overture', in *Dream on Monkey Mountain and Other Plays* (1972)

History we greed for in England,
Must know coolie ship, whip, brown paddy-skins
Burst, blown far by winds,
Whilst pearl-white rice feed overseer-mouth:
England, where it snows but we still born brown [...]

David Dabydeen, 'Homecoming,' from *Coolie Odyssey* (1988)

Import-export: the culture of the Caribbean

Not infrequently in the Caribbean, we hear complaints about 'cultural penetration' as a new form of imperialism. The region is swamped by imported television programmes, mainly of US origin. The youth listen more and more to rap rather than calypso or reggae, and seem more interested in basketball or soccer than in cricket. All this may be true, but it remains indisputable that culture and sport are among the Caribbean's most successful exports. The Amerindians gave the world tobacco, the hammock and the barbecue, and Amerindian elements feature prominently in the work of distinguished Caribbean artists such as the painter Aubrey Williams or the novelist Wilson Harris. However, much of the region's present day culture is the result of creolisation, the development of an

Traditional housing, St. Kitts   *John Gilmore*

intricate and uniquely Caribbean cultural pattern out of a wide range of elements, European, African, Asian, brought from other parts of the world.

The term creole derives from the Spanish *criollo* (apparently from *criar*, to create) which was originally used to distinguish colonists born in the New World from those born in Europe. It was later applied to slaves born in the Americas to distinguish them from 'salt-water' slaves imported from Africa, and, by extension, to any living thing originating in the plantation colonies, so that one could have creole horses or creole potatoes. With reference to human beings, it did not necessarily imply anything about race; one could have white, black or mixed creoles. However, the fact that it often came to be understood, especially by those from outside the region, as implying some degree of African ancestry, led to its disuse among some of the white Caribbean people to whom it had originally referred. In Guyana and Trinidad, creole came to be used to mean blacks as opposed to those of Indian ancestry (in the same way in which it is used in Mauritius), while in Belize it refers to blacks as opposed to mestizos, Garifuna and East Indians.

The history of the word begins to hint at the complexity which Caribbean societies owe to the process of creolisation, by which peoples of very different origins have been influenced both by their environment and by each other. The environmental influence can be seen in the traditional architecture of the region, in which both the plantation 'great house' with its thick stone

162

walls and high-ceilinged rooms, and the labourer's wooden cottage with its jalousied shutters and neat porch share a concern for protection from the sun as much as from the rain, for the need to take as much advantage as possible of any available breeze, and for an elegance of appearance which owes as much to an overall simplicity of design as to occasional touches of exuberant ornamentation in the way of gingerbread fretwork.

By contrast, a large part of the region's modern housing consists of buildings which are sited for the convenience of the developer anxious to get as many plots as possible out of the land available rather than to make the most sympathetic use of the location, and in which the architecture pays attention only to cost factors to the exclusion of any attempt at either elegance or convenience: relatively thin walls of cement blocks offering little protection against the heat are combined with windows designed and arranged so as to give minimal through ventilation.

The kitchen is an area in which the New World has had a wide-ranging and often forgotten influence. It is difficult to imagine Italian cooking without tomatoes, Indian or West African cooking without hot peppers, and West African cooking without the peanut or maize, yet all of these are American plants unknown in the Old World before the 16th century, like that other great American staple, the potato. Peanuts and hot peppers were important in the indigenous cooking of the Caribbean, but the region's staple was the cassava, which never became as widely diffused as the potato. European settlers in the Caribbean learnt the use of indigenous foods from the Amerindians, and the symbol of this process was the pepperpot, in which the essential ingredients were not only hot peppers but also cassareep, the concentrated juice of the bitter cassava which acted as a natural meat tenderiser and preservative, as well as giving the contents of the pot a characteristic flavour. As some was eaten, fresh ingredients could be added and the pot boiled up again and kept going in this manner for weeks or even months; there were stories of pepperpots handed down as heirlooms from generation to generation, and Aspinall claimed to have 'been privileged to partake of a 'pepper-pot' said to be over one hundred years old.'

Other dishes have more complicated cultural histories. Barbados' jug, or jug-jug, a dish made from guinea-corn (millet) flour, pigeon-peas, and minced beef and salt-pork, is said to derive from haggis – perhaps a tribute to those of the Highlanders defeated at Culloden who were exiled to the island – though a West African origin has also been suggested. Maize travelled from the Americas to West Africa, and then seems to have returned in a number of dishes. The most widely known is coucou (referred to as fungee or funchi in some parts of the Caribbean), which is essentially cornmeal boiled until stiff. Jamaicans, or at least some of them, regard it

Sauces and vegetables in the market, Tobago   *Pietro Cenini/Panos Pictures*

as fit only for feeding to your dog, but in Barbados flying fish and coucou is the national dish. A Bajan cook adds the cornmeal to water in which okras have been boiled, so that the resulting 'okra slush' gives a smoothness to the dish; Grenadians use coconut milk instead, and some places just use cornmeal and water. Cornmeal also features in a West African dish known in several parts of the Caribbean as conkies, dukunu or blue-drawers; it is combined with sugar, grated pumpkin, coconut and other ingredients, wrapped in a quailed banana or plantain leaf, and steamed. For some reason, this was long associated in Barbados with that particularly English festival, Guy Fawkes' Day (5 November), but since 1966 it has been shifted to Independence Day (30 November). In its turn, Asia has made its contribution to Caribbean cuisine. Roti (a type of pancake-like Indian bread, which in the Caribbean is wrapped round a filling such as curried potato or curried chicken in a manner not usual in India, where the bread is eaten as a separate accompaniment to the main dish) has become widely popular as a sort of fast food, not just among communities of Indian origin. Curried goat rivals ackee and salt-fish as Jamaica's national dish.

Music shows a similar creative interpenetration of influences. Seventeenth- and 18th-century slave-owners feared the power of African drumming, both as a means of signalling and of stirring up rebellious emotions, and made frequent unsuccessful attempts to ban it. At the same time, music and dancing were among the few recreations available to all

164

classes in colonial societies, and slaves were trained in the use of European instruments so they could provide orchestras for their masters' balls. Inevitably, slaves took to European dances like the quadrille and the waltz, while the whites developed a susceptibility to African rhythms. The violin survives as a folk instrument in some places, while in different islands a number of adaptations of the fife and drum bands of European regiments, such as the tuk band of Barbados and the 'big drum' of St. Kitts and Nevis, continue to perform creolised folk music. The combination of African rhythm with European-style use of melody is at the heart of much of Caribbean music, and some of its extraordinary versatility can be heard in the steel band. Trinidad's great gift to the world, this is claimed to be the only acoustic instrument invented in the 20th century. When the first pan appeared, sometime around the Second World War, it had only a few notes, but it was soon developed into the steel band of several pans of differing sizes offering a wide range of notes, so that it could be used to play everything from calypsos to arrangements of classical symphonies. In recent years, Trinidadian music, and Caribbean music in general, has incorporated influences from Indian musical traditions, such as tassa drumming. While many forms of Caribbean music have become widely known, the outstanding success has been reggae which has grown out of the impoverished neighbourhoods of Kingston, Jamaica, to become the universally recognised protest music of the oppressed – best symbolised, perhaps, by Bob Marley's invitation to perform at Zimbabwe's Independence Concert in 1980.

The history of Caribbean sport is in some ways another example of creolisation: the names of Garfield Sobers and Brian Lara remind us that the story of West Indian cricket is the classic one of the colonised beating the imperialist massa at his own game, but we should not forget the enthusiastic following which baseball enjoys in the Hispanic Caribbean, or the importance of Dominican Republic and Puerto Rican players to the professional game in the USA. The Caribbean has made its mark in other sports as well, such as the Cuban boxer Teófilo Stevenson's repeated Olympic triumphs, the successes of its track and field stars like Jamaica's Merlene Ottey, its consistent presence for many years among the leaders of professional body-building internationally, the Cuban José Raúl Capablanca's dominance of international chess in the 1920s, and the Barbadian Suki King's tenure of the world championship in draughts.

Pan musician, Trinidad

Betty Press/Panos Pictures

Exporting talent

Small countries are often exporters of talent to larger countries with greater opportunities. With a population of 133, 308, according to the 1991 census, St. Lucia has produced two Nobel prize-winners in the 20th century, but both Sir Arthur Lewis (1915-1991; Nobel Prize for Economics, 1979) and Derek Walcott (b. 1930; Nobel Prize for Literature, 1992) needed to work for much of their lives in other countries in order to achieve their success – so much so, in Lewis's case, that the *Encyclopædia Britannica* finds it possible to describe him as a 'British economist'.

The rise of Caribbean people to prominence in other parts of the world has been going on for a very long time. Born on the tiny island of Little Jost van Dykes in the British Virgin Islands, Dr. John Coakley Lettsom (1744-1815) became one of the most eminent physicians in England. In the 19th century, Barbados alone provided Britain with two diocesan bishops of the Church of England (as well as an Anglican bishop of Sierra Leone), an editor of the London *Times*, and the engineer who constructed St. Pancras Railway Station (then the largest span of any iron-roofed building in the world), as well as innumerable soldiers and administrators of all ranks throughout the British empire. The French colonial empire also provided opportunities for its Caribbean subjects: Alexis Saint-Léger. Léger (1887-1975), born in Guadeloupe, was a career diplomat as well as a poet (under the name Saint-John Perse) who won the Nobel Prize for Literature in

166

1960, while the colonial administrator Félix Éboué (1884-1944) from Cayenne played a major rôle in rallying French Equatorial Africa to De Gaulle's Free French during the Second World War – as a result he was not only made the territory's Governor-General but also eventually became the first black man to be buried in France's shrine to its national heroes, the Panthéon in Paris.

Colonial empires have been largely replaced by an international market economy. Changes in immigration laws have made large-scale movement of labour such as characterised the building of the Panama Canal or Caribbean migration to Britain in the 1950s a thing of the past. Nevertheless, doctors, academics and other professionals from the Caribbean find that their skills can still secure them jobs in extra-regional countries.

This is perhaps best seen in professional sport. The Caribbean has a wealth of sporting talent, and many Caribbean governments (with Cuba being the outstanding example) devote significant resources to fostering this. However it is still largely the case that the best training facilities and career opportunities have to be sought elsewhere. We see world-class athletes like Barbados' Obadele Thompson and Trinidad and Tobago's Ato Boldon spending much of their time living and training in the USA, while other Caribbean sports stars can make a good living playing for English soccer clubs or country cricket teams. Guadeloupe's Marie-José Perec runs for France.

In the case of the Dominican Republic and professional baseball, the export of talent has been turned into a highly organised and successful industry. US influence spread baseball to Mexico and the Caribbean from the late 19th century, and the game has long been extremely popular in Cuba, the Dominican Republic, Puerto Rico and Venezuela, though attempts to secure a following for it in the cricket-playing former British colonies have so far had little result. Baseball is a national sport in Cuba – Fidel Castro was regarded as a promising pitcher in his youth – and the high standard to which it is played there is shown by the way in which the Cubans won the gold medal for the game at both the Barcelona (1992) and Atlanta (1996) Olympics, beating off strong competition from US and Japanese teams. Cuba used to supply many professional players to the US major leagues, but this came to an abrupt end with the Castro revolution and the US embargo.

From the 1980s, when the Los Angeles Dodgers and the Toronto Blue Jays opened an experimental talent-spotting camp in the Dominican Republic, that country has become a major source of players for the professional game in North America. By 1999 there were 26 *academias de béisbol* in the DR, including one specialising in the supply of players to

Cricket, a popular game even in 1910, Barbados   *Courtesy of John Gilmore*

Japan.   More than 500 Dominicanos were playing in the professional
game in the US, including 70 in the major leagues, among them Pedro
Martínez, the highest paid player in the US.   The DR supplies more major
league players than any other country outside the US, well ahead of Puerto
Rico (42 in 1999), Venezuela and Mexico.   Other DR players work in
Venezuela, Japan, Taiwan and Korea.

The multi-million dollar salaries paid to the game's top players fire the
hopes of thousands of young DR baseball enthusiasts.   Most are
disappointed, though even those who are never signed by a US team but
still get as far as the Dominican Summer League can earn over US$600 a
month, a lavish income by local standards.   The remittances of those who
do make it abroad help to support relatives in their home towns and villages,
and when they return, temporarily or permanently, the money they bring
with them makes a significant contribution to the national economy.

Although few of them can hope for the sort of incomes achieved by the
stars of baseball, professionals from all over the Caribbean continue to earn
a living in many countries outside the region in many different walks of
life.   Few of them ever forget 'where they navel-string bury' and even if
they do not achieve the common ambition of retiring to their homeland,
they often help to support relatives there by sending cash or goods.   It is a
pattern which goes back at least to the middle of the 19th century.   In spite
of the enormous development which has taken place in the Caribbean in
the last fifty years, the fact that there is a limit to the number of jobs for
trained professionals in a small country means that it is a pattern which is
likely to continue well into the future.

168

Religion

Colonialism divided the Caribbean between Catholic and Protestant powers, but the slave trade and the indentureship system ensured a much more intricate picture. African religions like Orisha survive in Trinidad, while several parts of the region are home to faiths which have developed in the Caribbean out of African and Euro-Christian elements, of which Haiti's Vodun and Cuba's Santería are the best known. Hinduism and Islam in the Caribbean are predominantly religions of the East Indian communities, though they have not been without their influence on others. In spite of his reverence for the divinity of Haile Selassie and his emphasis on his African heritage, the Rastaman with his locks, his ganja and his belief in the importance of 'itals' (vegetarian food) and abstention from alcohol, owes more than a little to the Hindu sadhu. The Spiritual Baptist churches which have their origin in Trinidad and which have spread to Tobago, Barbados, Grenada and other parts of the region, offer an Afrocentric interpretation of Christianity couched in language which owes much to the King James version of the Bible, the Book of Common Prayer and Hymns Ancient & Modern, and expressed in a ritual which owes at least some of its elements to Hinduism. The 20th century has seen the widespread growth in the Caribbean of evangelical Christian denominations of North American origin. The history of Jewish communities in the Caribbean goes back to the 17th century, and a number of other faiths add to the general complexity.

During the slavery period, the civil and ecclesiastical authorities in Catholic colonies were usually concerned to ensure that slaves were baptised, but they were seldom offered the opportunity to gain a real knowledge and understanding of Christianity. Protestant colonies were often actively hostile to the Christianization of slaves. Protestant missions to slaves began in the early 18th century with the efforts of the Moravians in the Danish West Indies, from where they spread to other territories, to be followed by the Methodists and the Baptists, and, towards the end of the 18th century, the Anglicans (who had generally confined their attention to the white population of the islands) began to recognise that the slaves formed part of their care. However, persecution of black Christians and of white clergy who ministered to them occurred with some frequency until near the end of the slavery period, when slave-owners began to feel that religion and a modicum of education might be useful as means of social control. During slavery and for long afterwards, any manifestation of African religious beliefs and practices was likely to be condemned as heathenism and witchcraft and made subject to legal penalties. For example, the practise of the Spiritual Baptist faith was prohibited by law in Trinidad and Tobago between 1917

A modern mosque and an 18th century
synagogue, Paramaribo, Suriname

John Gilmore

and 1951, while in 1941-42, the Catholic Church and the government in Haiti conducted an 'anti-superstition campaign' which was an active persecution of vodun and its followers.

Jews faced a number of discriminatory policies until the 19th century, but in the Dutch and Danish colonies, in Jamaica and Barbados, they nevertheless found a greater freedom than was often possible in Europe. Much later, during the Nazi period, a number of Jewish refugees found homes in the Caribbean, reviving communities which had been declining in numbers. In the 19th century, Asian immigrants faced some religious discrimination: in Trinidad and Guyana, for example, Hindu and Muslim marriages were not officially recognised until the 20th century. With the relaxation in the 1990s of Cuba's official hostility to religion, however, the region as a whole has come to enjoy a widespread and high level of religious freedom. This is not always matched with ecumenical understanding – different faiths sometimes publicly attack each other's beliefs in a manner distinctly lacking in charity and humility – but intercommunal tensions based on religious differences are at a very low level compared to some parts of the world.

Any widespread interest in the education of the masses was generally the result of the approach of emancipation. While a privileged few were always given an education equal to whatever was considered the best in the 'mother country', even if it meant sending them to Europe for it, the education of the working-class child was usually based on the idea that it

170

Catholic and Anglican cathedrals, St Vincent   *John Gilmore*

should, as Richard Rawle (an English clergyman working in Barbados, who later became the first Anglican Bishop of Trinidad) put it in the mid-19th century, rid him of the 'conceit that he is too good for the hoe, and that industry has a suspicious relation to slavery.' Education was also largely dominated by the Christian churches – a particular problem for Indian immigrants, who feared that their children would be pressured into conversion. At the same time, it was intended to promote loyalty to the mother country – in the British colonies, for example, this meant not just Empire Day parades, but learning British literature, history and geography to the virtual exclusion of material with any Caribbean content.

Education

Most of this has changed with political and economic development. Caribbean countries devote very large proportions of their budgets to education, which is seen as promoting both national development and upward social mobility for individuals. Access to secondary and tertiary education has been greatly increased, and in some territories all children have the right to free education to the end of their secondary schooling and then to free university education if they meet the scholastic requirements. While the state has taken over much of the churches' role in the provision of education, there is at the same time a wider acceptance of religious education – in both non-Christian and Christian traditions – for those who wish it. Some problems remain because of lack of resources, but

171

national and regional institutions offer a generally high standard of education up to university level to most of the children of the Caribbean. At the same time, changes in policy and the work of organisations like the Caribbean Examinations Council and the University of the West Indies has made the curriculum much more responsive to local needs and culture.

This has included the formal teaching of Caribbean literature at school and university level. One effect of the region's history has been the development of creolised languages, whose vocabulary is largely drawn from the different languages of the colonising powers, but which share an underlying grammatical structure based on West African models. These were long despised as 'broken English,' 'français estropié,' 'gebroken Spans' or simply as 'dialect.' Even the name of the Papiamentu language originally carried the pejorative suggestion of chattering or babbling. They were cursed as languages which had been born in slavery – though in the early 19th century the wife of the governor of Jamaica noted how white upper-class Jamaican women spoke like their slaves.

The creole influence affected the speech of all classes and races; the distinctive Jamaican and Barbadian accents had both developed by the mid-18th century, if not earlier, and in Curaçao it was Papiamentu rather than the language of the Dutch rulers which came to provide a very varied population with some sense of unity. While there is still a widespread emphasis on the use of 'good,' 'correct' or 'standard' language, nationalism and independence has seen a much greater recognition of the variety, richness and possibilities of the ways in which Caribbean people actually speak. An important step forward has been the recognition of Haitian Creole as an official language.

'A state of mind'

Caribbean literature goes back a long way – Joaquín Balaguer starts his history of the literature of the Dominican Republic with Columbus. The writings of the earlier periods have much of interest, though they are often alien to modern tastes as a result of their elitist and racist outlook. It is in the 20th century that poets, novelists and playwrights begin to treat characters taken from the Caribbean people as a whole, rather than just from the elite, as suitable subjects for literature and not simply as exotic background, and to explore the literary possibilities of popular speech. The spread of education, which has created authors drawn from a much wider range of class and racial backgrounds, has inevitably encouraged this process and the way in which it engages in the eternal search for national identities. The results have been impressive, among them, the use of Afro-Cuban

Derek Walcott
Courtesy Faber

rhythms in the poetry of Nicolás Guillén, the interweaving of French and Creole in the fiction of Martinique's Patrick Chamoiseau, the celebration of Barbados and Bajan speech in the poetry and criticism of Kamau Brathwaite, the plays and poetry of Derek Walcott. The Prix Goncourt, the Booker Prize, the Nobel itself, have provided formal recognition of the success which Caribbean literature has achieved far beyond the region through this exploration of the languages and societies in which it is rooted.

Unfortunately it sometimes seems that the Caribbean's outstanding achievers find it easier to gain recognition abroad than at home, and some of the region's finest talent is scattered well beyond its shores. But perhaps the Caribbean has become a state of mind. It is many years now since the Jamaican poet and performance artist Louise Bennett commented on the fact that 'West Indies colonising England in reverse' and even then it was not a new phenomenon. The limited opportunities available at home have for a long time ensured that migration has been a feature of Caribbean life: movement within the region, to Panama, and places even further afield such as Brazil and Ecuador. Before the US tightened its immigration laws in the 1920s, many West Indians went to that country, and figures like the Jamaican poet and novelist, Claude McKay, contributed to the Harlem Renaissance, while the Caribbean continues to play a major part in the work of later American writers like Paule Marshall and Audre Lorde.

There had been Caribbean communities in Britain from a much earlier period, but the arrival of the *Empire Windrush* in 1948 with about 450 mainly Jamaican immigrants marked the start of a new wave of migration. The 'Lonely Londoners' of Sam Selvon's classic novel, who were always thinking of their return to the Caribbean, have given way to a community

173

Patrick Chamoiseau
Courtesy Granta Books

which, while still faced with the problems caused by persistent discrimination, has become a permanent one which has transformed many aspects of British society.

The 1950s also saw the development of Canada as a focus of Caribbean migration, while the Cuban Revolution provided an impetus for a new Hispanic Caribbean movement into the USA. Over the years, there have been many other strands of movement out of the Caribbean, ranging from Belizeans heading for Los Angeles, to Surinamese settling in the Netherlands.

Return migration

Endurance and struggle have secured a permanent place for communities and individuals of Caribbean origin and descent in many countries outside the region. In Britain at the end of the 20th century for example, problems remain, exemplified by the 1993 murder of the black teenager Stephen Lawrence in Britain, and the resulting official enquiry which condemned institutional racism in the police force. Few, however, still talk about Black British people as 'immigrants'. Both the 1970s rhetoric about 'repatriation' (particularly associated with the white politician Enoch Powell) and the once popular black protest slogan of 'Come what may, we're here to stay' are things of the past: the Black British have become part of the landscape and everyone takes it for granted that they are there to stay. They have changed the face of popular culture in Britain and can be found in

'Sweetness' and the artist, J. Hinkson, Trinidad   *Pietro Cenini/Panos Pictures*

most walks of life, including both Houses of Parliament and the country's government.

However, while their children and grandchildren are settled in Britain, a feature of the 1990s has been the growth in the number of the first generation of Caribbean immigrants who decide to return to the Caribbean when they retire. The experience is not always a happy one: they have been away for a long time, and sometimes find that the country in which they grew up has changed beyond all recognition, or that they themselves have adapted to British ways more than they thought and that they are now regarded as virtual foreigners in the land of their birth.

Caribbean governments, on the other hand, welcome 'returning nationals' as having a potentially valuable contribution to make and both Jamaica and Barbados, for example, have established special government units to assist their resettlement and offer concessions such as the right to import household effects and vehicles free of customs duties. Official figures for Barbados for the period March 1996 to February 1997 showed 432 returning nationals, and the figure for the following year was estimated at 740. The overall impact on the island's economy is difficult to assess, but the Central Bank of Barbados estimated remittances from overseas and returned nationals for 1996 at BDS$125 million (US$62.5 million) and for 1997 at BDS$149 million (US$74.5 million). These figures included items like pensions from overseas sources and money sent for house repairs,

175

Moko jumbies from Peter Minshall's carnival creation, Tapestry, 1997   *Trinidad Guardian*

but not funds brought in by nationals on holiday or sent as gifts to friends or relatives.

Ties between the Caribbean and people of Caribbean origin living outside the region are often strong, and Caribbean governments are coming to recognise this as a significant resource. In August 1999, for example, the Haitian government launched a 'Plan Tourisme-Diaspora'. It was estimated that there were some two million Haitians living abroad, and that significant numbers of them bought real estate in their country of origin and pumped money into the Haitian economy in other ways (such as sending money to support relatives), making money transfers totalling some US$300 million a year. The government hoped to revive the country's tourist industry (severely battered by the political turmoil of the 1980s and early 1990s) by encouraging them to return more often to their country of origin. If a minimum 50,000 such visitors a year could be achieved, it was estimated that this would benefit the national economy by an additional US$35 million or so each year.

Millions of people in other parts of the world are now aware of the Caribbean in a way which was never the case before. From the Notting Hill Carnival to Caribana in Toronto, Labour Day in Brooklyn to Calle Ocho in Miami, the Caribbean is highly visible. Tourists come from all over the world to 56 Hope Road, Kingston, to pay tribute to the memory of Bob Marley. In Britain and North America, people of Caribbean origin

176

have achieved prominence in politics, the media and arts, and in sport. Yet there is still a widespread ignorance, still too many people who think that Barbados is somewhere in Jamaica, too many who think of the Caribbean only when there is a well publicised crisis like the Brixton Riots or the Haitian boat people and who the rest of the time remain indifferent to the concerns of Caribbean people living in countries which seem too small and too far away to really matter, indifferent to the concerns of Caribbean people living just round the corner from them in the big cities of the north.

Further Reading

Beckles, Hilary McD., *Natural Rebels: A Social History of Enslaved Black Women in Barbados* (Zed Books, 1989)

Beckles, Hilary, and Verene Shepherd, editors, *Caribbean Slave Society and Economy* (Ian Randle Publishers Ltd., Kingston, Jamaica, 1991)

Beckles, Hilary, and Verene Shepherd, editors, *Caribbean Freedom: Economy and Society from Emancipation to the Present* (Ian Randle Publishers Ltd., Kingston, Jamaica, 1993)

Beckles, Hilary McD., and Brian Stoddart, editors, *Liberation Cricket: West Indies cricket culture* (Ian Randle Publishers Ltd., Kingston, Jamaica, 1995)

Boyce Davies, Carole, and Elaine Savory Fido, editors, *Out of the Kumbla: Caribbean Women and Literature* (Africa World Press, Inc., 1990)

Brown, Stewart, and John Wickham, editors, *The Oxford Book of Caribbean Short Stories* (Oxford University Press, 1999)

Brown, Stewart, editor, *Caribbean Poetry Now* (2nd edtion, Edward Arnold, 1992)

Burnett, Paula, editor, *The Penguin Book of Caribbean Verse in English* (Penguin Books, 1986)

Burton, Richard D. E., and Fred Reno, editors, *French and West Indian: Martinique, Guadeloupe and French Guiana Today* (Warwick University Caribbean Studies, Macmillan Caribbean, 1995)

Carrington, Sean, *Wild Plants of the Eastern Caribbean* (Macmillan Caribbean, 1998)

Cohen, J. M., editor and translator, *The Four Voyages of Christopher Columbus* (Penguin, 1969)

Colchester, Marcus, *Guyana, Fragile Frontier: Loggers, Miners and Forest Peoples* (Latin America Bureau, 1997)

Dabydeen, David, and Brinsley Samaroo, editors, *Across the Dark Waters: Ethnicity and Indian Identity in the Caribbean* (Warwick University Caribbean Studies, Macmillan Caribbean, 1996)

Donnell, Alison, and Sarah Lawson Welsh, editors, *The Routledge Reader in Caribbean Literature* (Routledge, 1996)

Dunn, Richard S., *Sugar and Slaves: The Rise of the Planter Class in the English West Indies, 1624-1713* (University of North Carolina Press, 1972)

Fernández-Armesto, Felipe, *Columbus* (Oxford University Press, 1991)

Gilmore, John, *Glimpses of our past: A social history of the Caribbean in postcards,* (Ian Randle Publishers, Kingston, Jamaica, 1995)

Gilmore, John, *The Poetics of Empire: A Study of James Grainger's* The Sugar-Cane *(1764)* (Athlone Press, 2000)

Hennessy, Alistair, editor, *Intellectuals in the Twentieth-Century Caribbean* (2 vols., Warwick University Caribbean Studies, Macmillan Caribbean, 1992)

Huberman, Leo, and Paul M. Sweezy, *Cuba: Anatomy of a Revolution* (Modern Reader paperback edition, Monthly Review Press, New York, 1968)

Hulme, Peter, *Colonial Encounters: Europe and the Native Caribbean, 1492-1797* (Methuen, 1986)

Hulme, Peter, and Neil L. Whitehead, editors, *Wild Majesty: Encounters with Caribs from Columbus to the present day* (Oxford University Press, 1992)

Lewis, Gordon K., *Main Currents in Caribbean Thought: The Historical Evolution of Caribbean Society in its Ideological Aspects, 1492-1900* (Johns Hopkins University Press, 1983)

López Springfield, Consuelo, editor, *Daughters of Caliban: Caribbean Women in the Twentieth Century* (Latin America Bureau, 1997)

Maingot, Anthony P., *The United States and the Caribbean* (Warwick University Caribbean Studies, Macmillan Caribbean, 1994)

Mohammed, Patricia, guest editor, *Rethinking Caribbean Difference*, special issue of *Feminist Review* (No. 59, Summer 1998)

Momsen, Janet H., editor, *Women and Change in the Caribbean* (Ian Randle Publishers Ltd., Kingston, Jamaica, 1993)

Moreno Fraginals, Manuel (translated by Cedric Belfrage), *The Sugar Mill: The Socioeconomic Complex of Sugar in Cuba, 1760-1860* (Monthly Review Press, 1976)

Murray, John A., editor, *The Islands and the Sea: Five centuries of Nature Writing from the Caribbean* (Oxford University Press, New York, 1991)

Nicholls, David, *From Dessalines to Duvalier: Race, Colour and National Independence in Haiti* (3rd edition, Warwick University Caribbean Studies, Macmillan Caribbean, 1996)

Patullo, Polly, *Last Resorts: The Cost of Tourism in the Caribbean* (Latin America Bureau, 1996)

Payne, Anthony, and Paul Sutton, editors, *Modern Caribbean Politics* (Ian Randle Publishers Ltd., Kingston, Jamaica, 1993)

Ridgeway, James, editor, *The Haiti Files: Decoding the Crisis* (Essential Books/Azul Editions, Washington, D. C., 1994).

Sauer, Carl Ortwin, *The Early Spanish Main* (University of California Press, 1966)

Watts, David, *The West Indies: Patterns of Development, Culture and Environmental Change since 1492* (Cambridge University Press, 1987)

Wilson, Mark, *The Caribbean Environment* (Oxford University Press, 1989)

Institute of Latin American Studies

31 Tavistock Square

London WC1H 9HA

Index